Fenland Waterways of the Middle Level

A guide for river users

ANDREW HUNTER BLAIR

with the assistance of the Middle Level Commissioners

> *Though there is nothing interesting in the country itself,*
> *by a concurrence of circumstances it then appeared very agreeable*
> Lord Orford's Voyage round the Fens in 1774

GW00514925

Imray Laurie Norie  Wilson

Published by
Imray, Laurie, Norie & Wilson Ltd
Wych House, The Broadway, St Ives,
Cambridgeshire PE27 5BT, England
☎ (01480) 462114 *Fax* (01480) 496109
Email ilnw@imray.com
www.imray.com
2012

Maps based on Ordnance Survey mapping
with the permission of The Controller of
Her Majesty's Stationery Office
© Crown Copyright INF 101177

British Library Cataloguing in
Publication Data.
A catalogue record for this book is available
from the British Library

ISBN 978 184623 440 8

CAUTION
Every effort has been taken to ensure the
accuracy of this book. It contains selected
information and thus is not definitive and
does not include all known information on
the subject in hand; this is particularly
relevant to the plans which should not be
used for navigation. The author and
publisher believe that its selection is a useful
aid to prudent navigation but the safety of a
vessel depends ultimately on the judgement
of the navigator who should assess all
information, published or unpublished,
available to him.

These notes are reproduced with permission
from *Navigations in the Anglian Region*,
published by the Environment Agency and
from *Middle Level Navigation Notes*
published by the Middle Level
Commissioners.

This work has been corrected to
February 2012

Printed by Sudbury Print Group, Suffolk, UK

Key to symbols used on the maps

Scale approximately 3]] to a mile

⚓	Moorings
⚓EA	Enviroment Agency
⚓GOBA	Great Ouse Boating Association
◣	Slipway
→	Direction of stream
✉	Post Office
☎	Telephone
⇒	Lock
═	Weir
𝒊	Information
🅽	Pump-out
WC	Toilet
⌑	Public House
🛢	Fuel
🚰	Water
✠	Church
⇌	Station
🚿	Showers
••••	Power Cable
- - - -	Footpath
GS	General Store
E.Cl.	Early Closing
F&C	Fish and Chips
U/S	Upstream
D/S	Downstream
M	Miles
km	Kilometres

Contents

Introduction, 4
  River Cruising, 4

The Middle Level, 5
  Points of entry, 5
  Navigation, 5
  Moorings, 5

The River Great Ouse and Nene, 6
  Authorities, 6
  Tides, 6
  Navigation, 6
  Environment Agency moorings, 7

Boat licensing and registration, 7

References and further reading, 8

Miscellaneous, 9
  Useful telephone numbers, 9
  Tourist information centres, 9
  Marinas, 9
  Toilet pump-out facilities, 9

Distances and dimensions, 9
  River Great Ouse to River Nene, 9
  Other navigable waterways, 10

River Great Ouse to River Nene, 11
  Salters Lode lock to Marmont Priory Lock, 11
  Marmont Priory Lock to Ashline Lock, 19
  Ashline Lock to Stanground Lock, 24
  Reed Fen Farm to Angle Bridge via the Twenty Foot River, 26

Other navigable waterways in the Middle Level, 29
  Flood's Ferry to Horseway lock, 29
  Wells Bridge to Holme Fen, 39

The Fens; past, present and future, 44
  The beginning, 44
  Early Fenland Rivers, 45
    Mankind's influence, 52
    The early days, 52
  Draining the Fens,
  The Middle Level today, 54
  The future, 54

Index, 56

Introduction

This guide describes the waterways of the Middle Level, an area of Fenland lying between Morton's Leam near the River Nene to the west and the Old Bedford River to the east and stretching from Wisbech in the north to Earith in the south. These waterways provide not only a unique drainage network but also a navigation link between the River Great Ouse near Denver and the River Nene at Peterborough and thence to the Grand Union Canal.

Following a description of the waterways, towns and villages, all rich in history and folklore, there is an explanation of the evolution of the Fenland and the development of its drainage system.

The Great Ouse, the New Bedford River, the land lying between and to the south of these two rivers (the South Level), the Nene and the land lying to the north (the North Level), are described only in so far as it is necessary to complete the account of the Middle Level.

The guide will be of interest not only to all river users, particularly navigators and walkers, but also to those who wish to explore the Fens.

River cruising

The Middle Level Commissioners maintain a system of waterways which provide arterial drainage and flood protection. Some of these are navigable and not only provide a through route between the River Great Ouse and the River Nene but also enable the Fenland Waterways to be explored. The Commissioners publish annually updated Navigation Notes which navigators are strongly recommended to obtain. The Environment Agency is generally responsible for the management of navigation on the River Great Ouse and River Nene. The laws, bylaws and regulations of both organisations are designed to ensure, as far as is reasonably practical, the safety and mutual enjoyment of the rivers by all.

River cruising is relaxing and enjoyable. The way of life should be unhurried, courteous and respectful of all other river users. A slow, sensible and considerate approach will help to maintain this tradition. Boat wash is perhaps the single most damaging aspect of river cruising. It can damage banks and passing and moored craft, cause injury and upset smaller craft. Watch the wash and slow down. There are some simple rules of the road.

- Keep to the speed limits
- Keep to the right when passing approaching craft
- Overtake on the left
- Never overtake near bends, bridges, approaching craft or moored craft
- Slow down and give way to sailing boats
- Slow down when approaching other craft, bridges and narrows
- Try to avoid anglers' fishing lines
- Be alert and keep a sharp lookout
- Use sound signals as required
  One short blast – I am steering to starboard
  Two short blasts – I am steering to port
  Three short blasts – My engines are going astern

In the Middle Level, short stay public moorings, usually free, are provided by the Fenland District Council, Parish Councils and the Well Creek Trust. On the Rivers Great Ouse and River Nene free moorings are provided by the Environment Agency, and in addition on the River Great Ouse, by the Great Ouse Boating Association (free to members). Other moorings are provided by certain local authorities and hotels and inns usually offer moorings to their patrons. Most marinas and some riparian owners provide moorings for a small charge. Here are some basic mooring guidelines.

- Do not leave it too late
- Moor facing upstream
- Do not allow mooring lines and stakes to form unforeseen hazards
- Always leave moorings clean and tidy

Locks, whilst being hazardous and requiring care, are often very sociable places and form part of the enjoyment of river cruising.

- Approach locks slowly
- If full or closed, moor at the landing stages
- Watch for currents, eddies and wind effects
- Follow any instructions – if in doubt seek help
- Ensure gates and paddles are in the correct positions before operation
- Always open paddles and gates slowly, a little at a time
- Before leaving upstream, close the upstream paddles
- Be alert and keep a sharp lookout

Explosion is the principal risk aboard. Petrol vapour can spread a long way and gas fumes can collect in the bottom of the boat.

- When refuelling, extinguish all naked lights and no smoking
- When changing gas bottles, turn off all appliances and no smoking
- Ensure that there are sufficient modern fire extinguishers
- Know where fire extinguishers and fire blankets are installed
- Know where the cabin exits are situated

For the comfort and safety of all on board, non-slip shoes should be worn and there should be a supply of dry, warm and waterproof clothes. Life-jackets should always be worn by children and non-swimmers.

- Know the location of life-belts
- Plan for and practise 'man overboard'
- Ensure that all on board know how to put the engine into neutral

The Middle Level

Authority

Middle Level Commissioners, Whittlesey Road, March, Cambridgeshire, PE15 0AH.
① 01354 653232
Fax 01354 659619
www.middlelevel.gov.uk

Points of Entry

The principal points of entry to the Middle Level Waterways are at Salter's Lode Lock from the River Great Ouse and at Stanground Lock from the River Nene. At least 24 hours notice should be given to the lock-keepers before entry to ensure adequacy of water levels (① 01366 382292 and 07824 600470 respectively). Welches Dam Lock and Horseway Lock are closed at present and the Forty Foot River is impassable east of Horseway Lock. There is therefore no access to the Old Bedford River at this point at present.

Navigation

No craft should be longer than 24·4m (80'), or wider than 3·0m (9'10") or have a draught greater than 0·7m (2'3"). Craft wider than 2·1m (6'10") and longer than 17·0m (55'9") may be restricted by the sharp bend at Whittlesey. If in doubt contact the lock-keeper at Stanground for advice, ① 07824 600470. Sudden strong currents due to pumping make navigation between Three Holes Bridge and Mullicourt Aqueduct on the Middle Level Main Drain/Sixteen Foot River inadvisable.

The Middle Level Commissioners publish annually updated notes entitled 'Middle Level Navigation Notes' on their website www.middlelevel.gov.uk. Potential navigators are strongly advised to obtain and read these carefully before attempting the passage. They are also advised to acquaint themselves with the Middle Level Bylaws, available from the Commissioners.

Moorings

Short stay moorings are available at:
Salter's Lode (Well Creek Trust)
Outwell Basin (Well Creek Trust)
Nene Parade, March (Fenland District Council)
Whittlesey Leisure Centre (Fenland District Council)
March Town Moorings (Fenland District Council)

Marylebone Bridge March (Fenland District
Council)
Benwick adjacent to cemetery (Benwick
Parish Council)
Whittlesey Leisure Centre (Fenland District
Council)

In addition moorings are available at
Marinas and at certain riverside inns for
patrons and a further short stay mooring is
proposed at Three Holes Road Bridge.

The River Great Ouse and River Nene

Authorities

The Environment Agency, Kingfisher House,
Goldhay Way, Orton Goldhay,
Peterborough, PE2 5ZR
℗ 08708 506506
www.environmentagency.gov.uk
Central Area, Bromholme Lane, Brampton,
Huntingdon, PE18 8NE
℗ 08708 506506
Northern Area, Waterside House, Waterside
North, Lincoln, LN2 5HA
℗ 08708 506506
Kings Lynn Conservancy Board, Common
Staithe Quay, King's Lynn
℗ 01553 773411
Associated British Ports, St Ann's Fort,
King's Lynn ℗ 01553 691555
Wisbech Port Manager, West Bank, Sutton
Bridge, Wisbech ℗ 01406 351530

Tides

High water at King's Lynn approx. 30 min
after Immingham. High water at Denver
approx. 1·75 hours after King's Lynn.
High Water at Sutton Bridge approx. 22 min
after Immingham. High water at Wisbech and
Dog in a Doublet approx. 40 min and 2 hours
20 min after Sutton Bridge respectively.

Navigation

Navigation on the tidal Great Ouse below
Denver, the tidal New Bedford River and the
tidal River Nene below Dog in a Doublet
should not be undertaken without local
knowledge and advice. Ebb and flood flows
can run fast and in a northerly wind, a bore
can accompany a spring flood tide. Craft
should proceed with great care through
Wisbech, where the banks are lined with steel
and concrete piles, the bed is stoned and
there are strong currents on both flood and
ebb tides. Large sea-going vessels navigate to
and from both Wisbech and Sutton Bridge.
Before entering any tidal river, navigators are
strongly recommended to contact the lock-
keeper at Denver ℗ 01366 382340, The
King's Lynn Conservancy Board ℗ 01553
773411, the lock-keeper at Dog in a Doublet
℗ 01733 202219, the lock-keeper at Salter's
Lode ℗ 01366 382292 or the Port Manager
at Sutton Bridge ℗ 01406 351133 as
appropriate.

To enter or leave the Middle Level waterways almost avoiding the tidal New Bedford River, where there can be either insufficient depth (0·3m at low springs and neap tides and 0·6m to 1m on high neap and spring tides respectively) or the headroom under bridges can be restricted at high tide, navigators should proceed from Earith via the Old West River to Popes Corner and the River Great Ouse to Denver where there is then only a short tidal stretch to Salter's Lode Lock, or vice versa.

To enter or leave the Grand Union Canal, craft should proceed via the River Nene from Stanground, through Northampton to Gayton, or vice versa.

Boat owners navigating the Middle Level Waterways should acquaint themselves with the Middle Level Bylaws, available from:

The Middle Level Commissioners, The Middle Level Offices, Whittlesey Road, March, PE15 0AH or on the Commissioners' website www.middlelevel.gov.uk

Boat owners navigating the recreational waterways within the Anglian Region of the Environment Agency should acquaint themselves with the following legislation, copies of which can be obtained from the Environment Agency in Peterborough.

The Recreational Waterways (Registration) Bylaws, 1979
The Recreational Waterways (General) Bylaws), 1980
The Recreational Waterways (Parks) Bylaws, 1981.

Environment Agency Moorings

Mooring on the tidal River Great Ouse, the tidal New Bedford River and the tidal River Nene is strongly inadvisable. Moorings at King's Lynn are by arrangement with Associated British Ports and on the River Nene below Bevis Hall by arrangement with the Port Manager at Sutton Bridge. Moorings on the non-tidal rivers are provided by the Environment Agency, The Great Ouse Boating Association, and Peterborough City Council.

The descriptions RH and LH refer to the banks as seen from craft cruising downstream.

Relief Channel

Downham Market LH bank at Collectors World (Environment Agency)
Stowbridge LH bank at Heron Public House (Environment Agency)
Magdalen Bridge LH bank at Cock Inn (Environment Agency)

River Great Ouse and Old West

Denver
LH bank upstream from Jenyn's Arms.
Silt Fen Farm
On RH bank 0·5km upstream from Denver Sluice.
Ten Mile Bank
Both banks upstream from Hilgay Bridge on River Great Ouse.
The Ship
On RH bank adjacent to the Ship Public House. (Environment Agency)
Brandon Creek
RH bank beside picnic area upstream from the Ship.
Littleport
Both banks between A10 road bridge and Littleport Boathaven.
Littleport
RH bank downstream from Sandhill's road bridge. (Environment Agency)
Diamond 44
On LH bank 0·25km upstream from junction with River Lark.
Queen Adelaide
RH bank immediately upstream from road and rail bridges.
Ely
Two moorings separated by the entrance to Bridge Boatyard on LH bank between the road and railway bridges, upstream from Ely Riverside. (Environment Agency)

The River Nene

Peterborough Town Quay, LH bank downstream of the Key Theatre.
Orton, RH bank upstream from Orton Lock

Note The descriptions RH and LH refer to the banks as seen from craft cruising downstream.

In addition marinas generally provide moorings for a small fee and certain Inns provide free moorings for patrons.

Further information

For the River Great Ouse see *The River Great Ouse and Tributaries* (Imray). For the River Nene see *The River Nene* (Imray). Further general information is published by the Environment Agency in *Navigations in the Anglian Region*.

Boat licensing and registration

No licence fees or tolls are presently levied by the Middle Level Commissioners on pleasure boats, although boats are required to have a current boat safety certificate. The name of each boat should, nevertheless, be clearly shown and visitors are required to register with the lock-keepers at Stanground or Salter's Lode, when entering the system. The majority of boat owners do so to gain access between its neighbouring river systems.

All craft using the River Great Ouse, the River Nene and associated waterways are obliged to be registered and to hold an up-to-date river licence.

Details of requirements for the registration and licensing of craft to the Environment Agency's controlled waterways are available from: The Environment Agency, Anglian Region, Kingfisher House, Goldhay Way, Orton Goldhay, Peterborough PE2 5ZR ☎ 08708 506506, from where details of the new arrangements relating to the Cam can be obtained.

References and further reading

The author gratefully acknowledges the following references and further reading, many of which have been extensively used as sources when researching the background to this guide.

A Geology for Engineers F G H Blyth. Arnold 1961

Geology and Scenery in England and Wales A E Trueman. Pelican 1963

The Cambridgeshire Landscape C Taylor. Hodder and Stoughton 1973. 0 340 15460 8

The Anglo Saxon Chronicle Trl. G N Garmonsway. Dent 1953

Roman Britain and Early England P Hunter Blair. Sphere Books 1975. 0 351 15318 7

Anglo Saxon England P Hunter Blair. Cambridge Univ. Press 1956

The Medieval Fenland H C Darby. David and Charles 1974. 0 7153 5919 3

Vermuyden and the Fens L E Harris. Cleaver Hume 1953

Lord Orford's Voyage Around the Fens Intr. H J K Jenkins. Cambs Library Publs 1987. 1 870724 7 04

The Fenland Past and Present S H Miller & S B J Skertchley. Longmans 1878

The Draining of the Fens H C Darby. Cambridge Univ. Press 1940

The Fens A Bloom. Robert Hale 1953

Fenland River R Tibbs. Dalton 1969. 900963 107

Portrait of the Fen Country E Storey. Hale 1972. 0 7091 24430

The Black Fens A K Astbury. E P Publishing 1973. 0 85409 605 1

The Great Ouse D Summers. David and Charles 1973. 0 7153 5971 1

Fenland Waterways M Roulstone. Balfour 1974

The Great Level D Summers. David and Charles 1976. 0 7153 7041 3.

The Changing Fenland H C Darby. Cambridge Univ. Press 1983. 0 521 24606 7

East Anglia D Wallace. Batsford 1939

East Anglia P Steggall. Robert Hale 1979. 0 7091 7398 9

Cambridgeshire A Mee. Hodder and Stoughton 1939

Cambridgeshire E A R Ennion. Robert Hale 1951

The Buildings of England, Cambridgeshire N Pevsner. Penguin 1954

A View of Cambridgeshire M Rouse. Dalton 1974. 900963 46 8

Cambridgeshire N Scarfe. Faber and Faber 1983. 0 571 13250 2

Suffolk and Norfolk M R James. Dent 1930

Norfolk A Mee. Hodder and Stoughton 1940.

The Buildings of England, NW&S Norfolk N Pevsner. Penguin 1962

Norfolk Villages D H Kennett. Robert Hale 1980. 0 7091 8129 9

Bedfordshire and Huntingdonshire A Mee. Hodder and Stoughton 1973. 0 340 15156 0

A History of Huntingdonshire M Wickes. Phillmore 1985. 0 85033 581 7

The Skaters of the Fens A Bloom. Heffer 1958

Cambridgeshire Customs and Folklore E Porter. Routledge & Kegan Paul 1969. 7100 6201 X

Forgotten Railways of East Anglia R S Joby. David and Charles 1977. 0 7153 7312 9

Maps

British Geological Survey. England and Wales, Solid and Drift
Sheet 158 Peterborough (1984)
Sheet 159 Wisbech (1995)
Sheet 172 Ramsey (1995)
Sheet 173 Ely (1980)
Sheet 188 Cambridge (1981)

Ordnance Survey Explorer 1:25,000
227 Peterborough
228 March and Ely
235 Wisbech and Peterborough North
236 King's Lynn, Downham Market and Swaffham

Miscellaneous

Useful telephone numbers

King's Lynn Conservancy Board, Common Staithe Quay, King's Lynn, ☎ 01553 773411

Associated British Ports, St Ann Fort, King's Lynn ☎ 01553 691555

Wisbech Port Manager, West Bank, Sutton Bridge, Wisbech ☎ 01406 351530

Great Ouse Boating Association, PO Box 244, Huntingdon, PE29 6FE
Email membership@goba.org.uk

Tourist information centres

Ely, Oliver Cromwell's House, 29 St. Mary's Street, Ely, Cambs. CB7 4HF
☎ 01353 662062

Peterborough, 45 Bridge Street, Peterborough ☎ 01733 452336

Marinas

Bill Fen Marina, Ramsey High Lode, Ramsey, Cambridgeshire
☎01487 813621

Ely Marine Ltd, Cathedral Marina, Waterside, Ely, Cambridgeshire
☎ 01353 664622

Fox Narrowboats, 10 Marina Drive, March, Cambridgeshire
☎ 01354 652770

Hermitage Marina, Earith, Huntingdon, Cambridgeshire ☎ 01487 840994

Oundle Marina, Oundle, Peterborough PE8 5PA ☎ 01832 272762

Peterborough Boating Centre, 73 North Street, Stanground, Peterborough
☎ 01733 566688

Popes Corner Marina, Holt Fen, Little Thetford, Ely, Cambridgeshire
☎ 01353 649580

West View Marina, High Street, Earith, Huntingdon ☎ 01487 841627

For details of all other marinas on the River Great Ouse and the River Nene, see *The River Great Ouse and Tributaries* (Imray) and *Map of the River Nene* (Imray), respectively

Toilet pump-out facilities

River Great Ouse
Denver Sluice, (Environment Agency)
Ely Willow Walk (Environment Agency)
Westview Marina (Environment Agency)
River Nene
Peterborough Town Quay, LH bank downstream of the Key Theatre.

Distances and dimensions

All dimensions are subject to the prevailing weather, tides, fresh water discharges and pumping conditions. They should therefore be treated only as a guide. Bridges, except for those listed, generally have a minimum head room of 2·5m (8'2").

River Great Ouse to River Nene

Distances	Km	(miles)
River Great Ouse		
Denver Sluice to:		
Salter's Lode Lock	0·5	(0·3)
Middle Level Recommended Link Route		
Salter's Lode Lock to:		
Well Creek		
Nordelph Road Bridge	3·0	(1·8)
Mullicourt Aqueduct	6·3	(3·9)
Outwell, St Clement's Bend	8·3	(5·2)
River Nene Old Course		
Marmont Priory Lock	12·0	(7·5)
Popham's Eau, Low Corner	14·3	(8·9)
Reed Fen, Twenty Foot	17·2	(10·7)
March Town Bridge	20·8	(12·9)
Fox Narrowboats	22·4	(13·9)
Staffurth's Bridge	27·1	(16·8)
Flood's Ferry Bridge	28·4	(17·6)
Whittlesey Dyke		
Angle Bridge	33·8	(21·0)
Turningtree Bridge	36·3	(22·6)
Briggate River		
Ashline Lock	37·5	(23·3)
Briggate Bend	38·1	(23·7)
King's Dyke		
Field's End Bridge (A605)	41·1	(25·5)
Stanground Lock	44·5	(27·7)
Stanground Lock to River Nene	0·9	(0·6)

Headroom under Bridges

Well Creek		
Nordelph Pipe & Road Bridge	2·3m	(7'6")
White House Farm Bridge	2·2m	(7'3")
Mullicourt Aqueduct (East)	2·1m	(6'11")
Mullicourt Aqueduct (West)	2·2m	(7'3")
River Nene Old Course		
Upwell Footbridge 1	2·3m	(7'6")
Upwell Roadbridge	2·2m	(7'3")
Upwell Footbridge 2	2·2m	(7'3")
Upwell Roadbridge B1412	2·3m	(7'6")
Upwell Footbridge 3	2·4m	(7'10")
Marmont Priory Lock	2·4m	(7'10")

Whittlesey Dyke

Burnthouse Farm Bridge	2·1m (6'11")
Angle Bridge	2·4m (7'10")

Locks

It is emphasised that the following dimensions should be treated as a guide. If the vessel's dimensions approach those listed above, navigators must proceed with extreme caution.

Great Ouse/Well Creek
Salter's Lode
Attended ☎ 01366 382292
Length 18·9m (62') *Width* 3·8m (12'5")
Possible passage for craft up to 24·3m (80') on level water and when tidal conditions allow.

River Nene Old Course
Marmont Priory
Attended part time ☎ 07824 821737
Length 28·0m (91'10") *Width* 3·65m (11')
In absence of lock-keeper, navigators should lock through themselves. Care must be taken to keep clear of upstream sill and the downstream access walkway.

Whittlesey Dyke
Ashline
Unattended
Length 27·4m (89'11") *Width* 3·5m (11'6")
Hold boats at least 1m (3'3") clear of upstream doors to avoid sill and away from downstream doors to avoid entrapment under walkway.

King's Dyke/River Nene
Stanground
Attended ☎ 07824 600470
Length 24·4m (80') *Width* 3·5m (11'6")
Maximum draught of boats longer than 11·0m (36'); 0·69m (2'3").

Notes
Maximum speed 8kmh (5mph) except between Salter's Lode Lock and Marmont Priory Lock and between Stangroud Lock and Turningtree Bridge where the maximum speed is 6·4kmh (4mph).

Sharp bend at Whittlesey restricts narrow boat length to 21·3m (70').

Keys for sanitation station (closed at present) and Ashline and Lodes End Lock security compounds are available from Salter's Lode Lock, Stanground Lock, Middle Level Offices, Fox Narrowboats and Bill Fen Marina. (£2.00).

Other navigable waterways

Distances	Km	(miles)
Popham's Eau		
Low Corner to		
Three Holes	3·5	(2·2)
Sixteen Foot Drain		
Forty Foot River	18·8	(11·7)
Twenty Foot River		
Reed Fen to		
Angle Bridge	16·1	(10·0)
River Nene Old Course		
Flood's Ferry Bridge to:		
Benwick	4·4	(2·7)
Wells Bridge	10·5	(6·5)
Ashline Lock	12·0	(7·5)
Nightingale's Corner	16·6	(10·3)
Nightingale's Corner to limit of navigation at:		
Great Raveley Drain		
Jackson's Bridge	2·7	(1·7)
Monk's Lode		
Conington Pumping Station	4·0	(2·5)
New Dyke		
GNER Crossing	4·7	(2·9)
Bevill's Leam		
Bevill's Leam Pumping Station	4·6	(2·8)
New Cut/Black Ham		
GNER Crossing	10·0	(6·2)
Ramsey High Lode		
Ashline Lock to:		
Bill Fen Marina	0·6	(0·4)
Ramsey Town	1·8	(1·1)
Forty Foot/Vermuyden's Drain		
Wells Bridge to:		
Puddock Bridge	5·1	(3·2)
Leonard Child's Bridge	8·3	(5·2)
Sixteen Foot Drain	12·3	(7·6)
Horseway Lock	13·8	(8·6)
Welches Dam Lock	17·3	(10·7)
(currently closed)		
Old Bedford River		
Welney Road Bridge	27·1	(16·8)
Old Bedford Sluice	36·4	(22·6)

Headroom under Bridges

Twenty Foot River		
Infields Bridge	1·6m	(5'3")
Poplar Tree Bridge	2·4m	(7'10")
Angle Bridge	2·4m	(7'10")
River Nene Old Course		
White Fen Farm Bridge	2·3m	(7'6")
Exhibition Bridge	1·2m	(3'11")
New Cut		
Herbert's Bridge	2·2m	(7'3")

Forty Foot/Vermuyden's Drain
Ramsey Hollow Bridge   1·5m   (5')
Welches Dam   2·1m   (6'11")
(currently closed)

Locks

It is emphasised that the following dimensions should be treated as a guide. If the vessel's dimensions approach those listed above, navigators must proceed with extreme caution.

River Nene Old Course
Lode's End
Unattended
Length 20·7m (67'11") *Width* 3·3m (10'10")
Boats must be kept clear of the low-side access walkway to avoid entrapment· It is necessary to open the security fence gateway to navigate the lock.

Forty Foot/Vermuyden's Drain
Horseway
Unattended
Length 18·3m (60') *Width* 3·65m (12')
(currently closed)

Welches Dam
Unattended
Length 14·3m (47') *Width* 3·35m (11')
(currently closed)

River Great Ouse to River Nene

Recommended Link Route
Salter's Lode to Stanground Lock
Not only do the Middle Level waterways provide for irrigation, land drainage, flood defences and angling, but they provide fascinating and at times challenging navigable routes between the rivers Great Ouse and Nene. The recommended route through the Middle Level, about 46km long, starts at Salter's Lode lock and continues west along Well Creek past Nordelph to Outwell. Here it joins the River Nene (Old Course) southwest through Upwell and March to Flood's Ferry where it turns west again along the Whittlesey Dyke to Whittlesey. The final stretch from Whittlesey to Stanground is along the King's Dyke.

Salter's Lode Lock to Marmont Priory Lock

When Vermuyden built the Old Bedford River in 1637, he required two sluices to be built. One was of stone on the Old Bedford River itself, built to keep the tidal water out. The entrance to the Old Bedford River through its modern successor is on the western bank of the tidal River Great Ouse some 600m downstream from Denver Sluice (see Horseway to Old Bedford Sluice). The second, according to Dougdale, was a 'great sasse on Welle Creeke' (sasse – lock). The present lock dates from 1827 and cost around £7,000 to build. Its narrow entrance, also on the western bank of the Ouse is just a short distance downstream from the Old Bedford Sluice. The lock has a guillotine gate on the tidal side, guarded by a fine pair of stone eagles. A minor road bridge and footpath cross the lock pen and pointing doors give access to Well Creek. There is a landing stage on the north bank of the tidal entrance and landing stages and moorings on Well Creek (Middle Level Commissioners in connection with lock passage and Well Creek Trust).
Note Great care should be taken when navigating the tidal section of the Great Ouse and when entering or leaving the tidal side of Salter's Lode Lock.
Salter's Lode is a small fenland hamlet with no facilities. The nearest inn is the Jenyn's Arms on the west bank of the Great Ouse just upstream of Denver Sluice, where there are moorings, bar meals, a restaurant and accommodation.

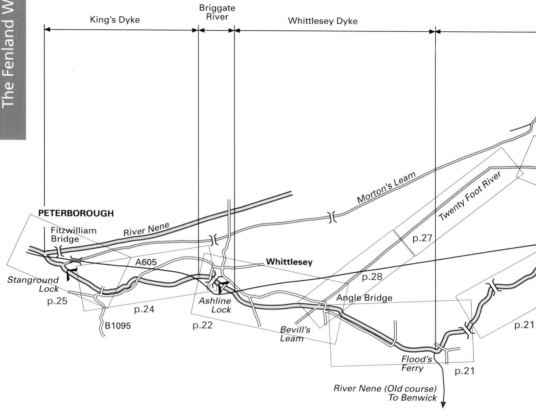

King's Dyke

Briggate
River

Whittlesey Dyke

Morton's Leam

Twenty Foot River

PETERBOROUGH

Fitzwilliam
Bridge

River Nene

p.27

Whittlesey

A605

Stanground
Lock

p.25

p.28

p.24

Ashline
Lock

Angle Bridge

p.21

B1095

p.22

Bevill's
Leam

Flood's
Ferry

p.21

River Nene (Old course)
To Benwick

N

RIVER OUSE TO RIVER NENE
Recommended Route

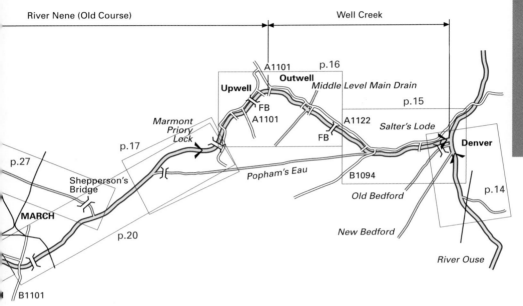

River Nene (Old Course)

Well Creek

p.16

A1101

Outwell

Upwell

Middle Level Main Drain

FB

p.15

A1101

A1122

Salter's Lode

Marmont
Priory
Lock

FB

Denver

p.17

p.27

Popham's Eau

B1094

p.14

Shepperson's
Bridge

Old Bedford

MARCH

New Bedford

p.20

River Ouse

B1101

```
0         1         2         3         4    Miles
├────┬────┼────┬────┼────┬────┼────┬────┤
0    1    2    3    4    5    6    Km
```

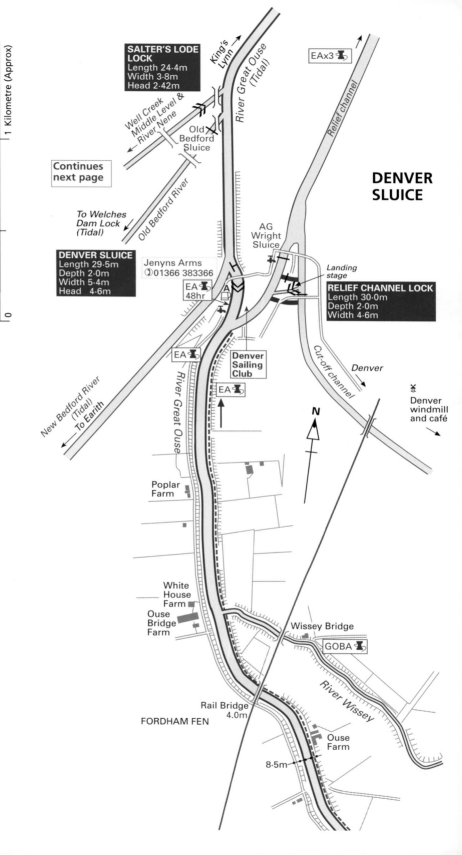

Mile 1

1 Kilometre (Approx)

0

0

SALTER'S LODE LOCK
Length 24·4m
Width 3·8m
Head 2·42m

King's Lynn

River Great Ouse (Tidal)

EAx3

Well Creek Middle Level & River Nene

Old Bedford Sluice

Continues next page

Old Bedford River

To Welches Dam Lock (Tidal)

DENVER SLUICE
Length 29·5m
Depth 2·0m
Width 5·4m
Head 4·6m

Jenyns Arms
☏ 01366 383366

EA 48hr

DENVER SLUICE

AG Wright Sluice

Landing stage

RELIEF CHANNEL LOCK
Length 30·0m
Depth 2·0m
Width 4·6m

Relief channel

EA

Denver Sailing Club

EA

New Bedford River (Tidal)
To Earith

River Great Ouse

Cut-off channel

Denver

N

Denver windmill and café

Poplar Farm

White House Farm

Ouse Bridge Farm

Wissey Bridge

GOBA

River Wissey

Rail Bridge 4.0m

FORDHAM FEN

Ouse Farm

8·5m

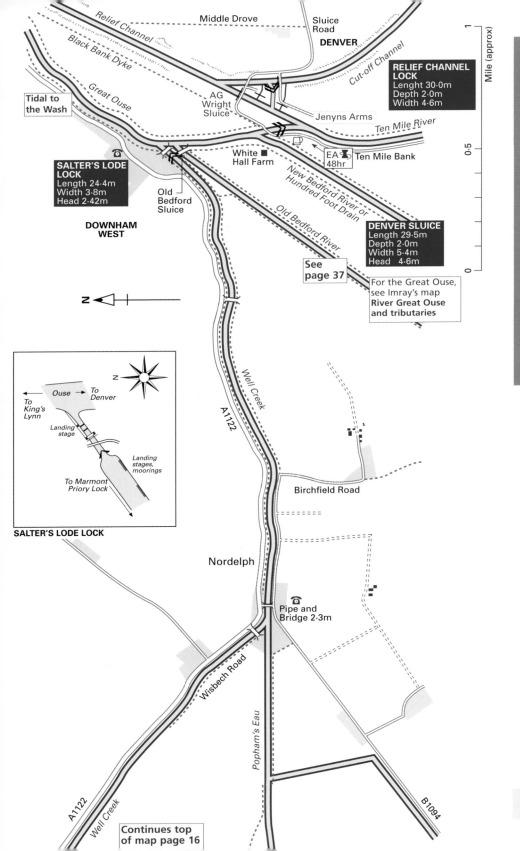

Middle Drove

Relief Channel

Sluice Road

DENVER

Black Bank Dyke

Cut-off Channel

Mile (approx)

1

RELIEF CHANNEL LOCK
Lenght 30·0m
Depth 2·0m
Width 4·6m

Great Ouse

AG Wright Sluice

Jenyns Arms

Ten Mile River

Tidal to the Wash

0.5

White Hall Farm

EA 48hr

Ten Mile Bank

☎

SALTER'S LODE LOCK
Length 24·4m
Width 3·8m
Head 2·42m

Old Bedford Sluice

New Bedford River or Hundred Foot Drain

DOWNHAM WEST

Old Bedford River

DENVER SLUICE
Length 29·5m
Depth 2·0m
Width 5·4m
Head 4·6m

See page 37

0

For the Great Ouse, see Imray's map **River Great Ouse and tributaries**

N

Well Creek

A1122

SALTER'S LODE LOCK

N

Ouse →
To Denver

← To King's Lynn

Landing stage

Landing stages, moorings

To Marmont Priory Lock

Birchfield Road

Nordelph

☎ Pipe and Bridge 2·3m

Wisbech Road

Popham's Eau

A1122

Well Creek

B1094

Continues top of map page 16

15

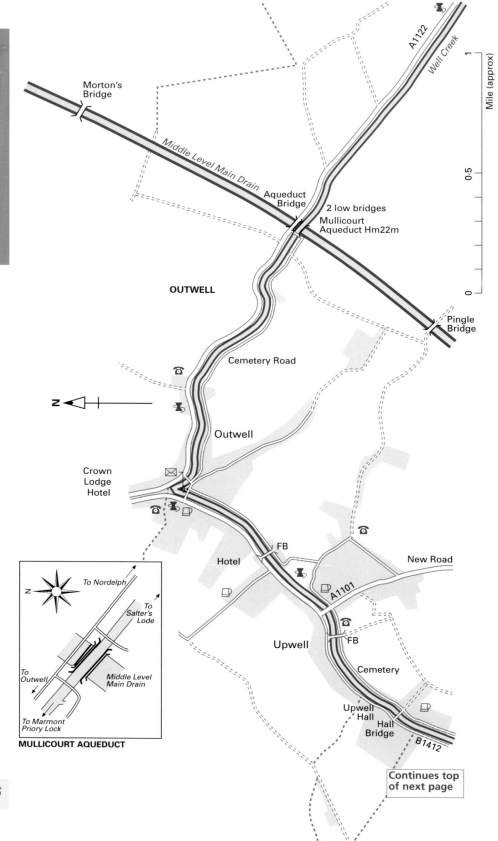

Morton's Bridge

A1122

Well Creek

Middle Level Main Drain

Aqueduct Bridge

2 low bridges
Mullicourt Aqueduct Hm22m

Mile (approx)

1

0.5

0

OUTWELL

Pingle Bridge

Cemetery Road

N

Outwell

Crown Lodge Hotel

FB

Hotel

New Road

A1101

Upwell

Cemetery

FB

Upwell Hall

Hall Bridge

B1412

MULLICOURT AQUEDUCT

N

To Nordelph

To Salter's Lode

To Outwell

Middle Level Main Drain

To Marmont Priory Lock

Continues top of next page

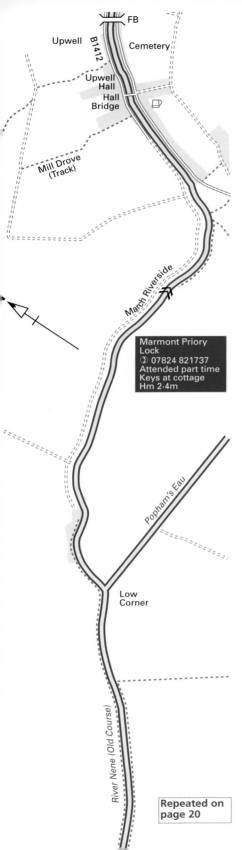

Marmont Priory
Lock
☎ 07824 821737
Attended part time
Keys at cottage
Hm 2·4m

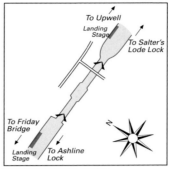

MARMONT PRIORY LOCK

Repeated on
page 20

Note The Jenyn's Arms cannot be directly accessed on foot from Salter's Lode.

Between Salter's Lode and Nordelph, Well Creek lies first in its natural ancient channel before entering, just east of the second bridge and near a 'pillbox', an artificial and probably Roman stretch. To the north is a footpath and a high flood bank below which is the busy A1122. To the south a low flood bank affords views over Fenland which drops away from the river. There is a bridle path, which forms the eastern part of the Well Creek Trust Nature Trail (for information contact David Barnard ☎ 01945 772041) and then a minor road leading to Nordelph. The Roman Fen Causeway linking Caistor in Norfolk with Peterborough, runs parallel to and about 0·5km to the south of the river.

The area around Nordelph was important not only in Roman times, when it developed into a Romano-British village lying between the Roman Fen Causeway and the artificial link joining the two ancient branches of Well Creek, but also between the mid-16th century and mid-19th century when it was at a key point in a network of fen drains. Popham's Eau ran straight from the Old River Nene just north of March via Three Holes to Nordelph thus bypassing the much longer route through Upwell and Outwell. It conveyed water from the River Nene and, after the Sixteen Foot Drain had been cut (1651), water from some of the southern part of the Middle Level. Once at Nordelph these waters either flowed east to the Ouse at Salter's Lode or along Tong's Drain (1653), a relief channel which ran northeast to join the Ouse near Stow Bridge. This drain is now extinct having been made redundant when the Middle Level Main Drain was cut in 1848.

The river's willow tree lined banks are well kept and are particularly attractive in the spring when they are covered with daffodils. A few houses and a former windmill border Well Creek and on the north bank there is a garage and the Chequers public house (bar meals), between which Tong's Drain would have flowed. There is a small car park near the bridge, convenient for the Well Creek Trust nature trail. Holy Trinity Church dates from 1865, before which parishioners are said to have travelled in a horse drawn barge to churches at Outwell and Upwell. Victoria Chapel (1861) formerly a Wesleyan Chapel, is now a private riverside house. West of the road bridge, Popham's Eau (navigable between Nordelph Pumping Station and Three Holes but no turning area) continues westwards whilst Well Creek turns northwest towards Outwell.

After a relatively straight stretch (4km), half way along which is a footbridge, Well Creek, still bordered on the north by a footpath (the western part of the Well Creek Trust nature trail), a high bank and the A1122, flows over the Middle Level Main Drain in Mullicourt Aqueduct. Built in 1848 and lying between a modern concrete bridge and an older 'Cock Up' bridge, this iron aqueduct is named after Mullicourt Priory. Although no trace of the Priory remains, it was probably a 10th-century Benedictine Priory annexed to Ely. The Middle Level Main Drain (1848), an extension of the Sixteen Foot Drain, flows in a straight line northeast for 11km towards the Ouse near King's Lynn; navigation is prohibited north of Mullicourt. The 'Cock Up' bridge (weight limit three tonnes) gives access to the Well Creek Trust slipway, limited parking and a pleasant minor road which follows the south bank of the river for 2km to Outwell.

Outwell and Upwell form in effect one long village bordering both sides of the western end of Well Creek, part of the now extinct Wisbech Canal and the Old River Nene, which forms the county boundary between Cambridgeshire and Norfolk. Built on silt and once described as the longest village in England, its name is derived from the Anglo-Saxon settlement of Well, Welle or Welles. The northern part became known as Outwell, where the river flowed out of the village and the southern part, Upwell, the upstream end.

Well Creek, narrow here, flows into Outwell through orchards, between well-kept banks with willow trees and in the spring lined with daffodils. The modern Crown (sports facilities) is at the east end of Outwell on the north bank on which thereafter lie generally older houses. At the centre of the village, Well Creek joins the old course of the River Nene, the channel flowing past the Red Lion Inn and around the Parish Church of St Clement, turning

through almost 360°. At the apex of the bend, where there are moorings, the Old River Nene and then the Wisbech Canal flowed north past Beaupré Hall (1525) and Beaupré Hall Farm, a red-brick Jacobean house with stepped gable ends. Although the old river and canal are now extinct, their course lay between the A1122 and A1101, where there are remains of sluices (1795?).

The Parish Church of St Clement, the third Bishop of Rome, who allegedly was banished to the Crimea which he converted to Christianity before being drowned with an anchor tied around his neck, is built of Barnack stone and dates from the mid-13th century. The roof of the 14th-century nave appears to be supported by angels with red wings, one of which carries a scroll inscribed with an anchor for St Clement. There is a massive 15th-century iron-bound chest, a good brass of a figure in armour commemorating Richard Quadryng who died in September 1511 and 16th-century memorials to the Beaupré family.

In the village by the church and the road bridge (1682) across the river are the Crown Inn, an off-licence and post office, a general stores and a fish and chip shop.

Moving into Upwell, the River Nene (Old Course) still lies in a narrow channel between well-kept tree-lined banks which gradually give way to private gardens and moorings on the east and open fenland to the west. On the west bank are some elegant Georgian houses, a number of shops including a butcher, general store, baker, post office and a branch of Lloyd's Bank as well as the recently refurbished Old Mill Hotel (restaurant, accommodation and moorings). The Five Bells (restaurant, accommodation, bar meals,) is on the east bank near St Peter's Parish Church and further along, by a footbridge and where the river turns west away from the village, is the Globe Inn (moorings, bar meals) and an award winning fish and chip shop.

St Peter's Church, much restored in 1836 and 1842, dates from the 13th century. Like Outwell it is built of Barnack stone and also has its roof apparently supported by angels with spread wings on the hammer beams which alternate with tie beams. The porch with a vaulted ceiling and upper room, is decorated with sixteen pelicans. Inside the church are two early-15th-century brasses, a finely carved royal coat of arms and a salutary memorial to 67 parishioners who died between 21st June and 13th August 1832 from 'Asiatic Cholera', a frightful and previously unknown disease in this country. The brick-built house immediately to the south of the church, once used as the rectory, dates from around 1525.

Upwell was the terminus of the former Wisbech and Upwell Tramway, a standard-gauge light railway built by the Great Eastern Railway Company, opened between Wisbech and Outwell on 20th August 1883 and extended to Upwell on 3rd September 1884. Trains of little tram-like carriages with 'balconies' at each end were hauled by small squat four-wheeled tank engines which had been fitted with protective wooden side-plates which partially covered the wheels and motion (to avoid frightening horses!), small chimneys, cowcatchers and bells. Rather like steaming guards' vans, they became the subject of one of the Rev. W Audrey's children's railway books, *No.7 Toby the Tram Engine*. The maximum speed for the 40-minute 10km journey was between 19kph and 4·5kph when crossing roads at Outwell and indeed governors were fitted to cut off the steam at 19kph. There was a regular passenger service until New Year's Eve 1927 and as well as the frequent stopping places, passengers could stop the train anywhere by simply flagging it down. Steam engines continued to haul the goods service until they were replaced by diesel engines, also fitted with cowcatchers and side-plates, in 1952. The tramway finally closed on 23rd May 1966 and now only a few traces remain in Outwell.

At the southern end of Upwell the road continues to Three Holes (the Red Hart public house (now closed), PO and stores, garages), situated at the junction of Popham's Eau and the Sixteen Foot Drain/Middle Level Main Drain. Here, new public short stay moorings are proposed. The eastern part of Popham's Eau from Nordelph Pumping Station to Nordelph was, like Tong's Drain, made redundant by the cutting of the Middle Level Main Drain (1848) and is unnavigable. The western part which runs in a straight 3·5km channel to the River Nene (Old Course) is navigable, but is of limited interest. Whilst the Middle Level Main Drain is navigable as far as Mullicourt Aqueduct, it is not recommended due to sudden pumping and sluicing operations. The Sixteen Foot Drain is also navigable southwards to Vermuyden's Drain, however it runs in a deep straight channel for some 15km and apart from occasional road bridges, farm access bridges and at Stonea, a railway bridge with the neighbouring Golden Lion public house, there is little to relieve the monotony. Nevertheless about 1km to the west and accessed from the B1093 via Stitches Farm is an ancient site consisting of Stonea Camp, a restored Iron Age 'Hill' (!) Fort, a tumulus and the site of a Roman settlement.

However south of Three Holes, east of the Sixteen Foot Drain and lying close to the bed of the Old Croft River is the small village of Christchurch where Dorothy Sayers was born. Her father, Henry Sayers, was rector of the small red-brick cruciform church and she used the fenland setting for her detective story, *The Nine Taylors* (1934). In the village there are a stores, an off-licence, a post office and the Dun Cow public house.

On leaving Upwell, the River Nene (Old Course) turns west towards Marmont Priory Lock. After deep ploughing, there is now no trace of the Gilbertine Priory, founded in 1204, named after Marmonde on the River Gironde in France and which lay just to the north of the lock. The recently enlarged lock (28m) is usually manned ☏ 07824 821737 and navigators are encouraged to double up whenever possible to assist maintaining an adequate water level in the eastern part of the River Nene (Old Course) and in Well Creek.

Marmont Priory Lock to Ashline Lock

To the west of Marmont Lock the River Nene (Old Course) continues in a narrow deep channel, bordered on the north bank as far as Laddus Farm by a public road, to its junction with Popham's Eau at Low Corner, after which it enters a much wider channel. Laddus farm is private, and although there is a public footpath on the north bank which leads, after a detour of about 1km to cross the Twenty Foot River at Shepperson's Bridge, to March, it is virtually impassible. The Hereward Way, a long-distance footpath between Ely and Peterborough, joins the river on the south bank and there is a good path, made up in places, from Euximoor (15th century Yekeswellemoor, 'The marsh by the Cuckoo's Spring or Stream') past Reed Fen Pumping Station, Reed Fen Farm and the railway bridge to the outskirts of March where it crosses the river to join a minor road on the north bank. From Reed Fen Farm there are two routes to Whittlesey, one via the Twenty Foot River north around March and the second, the preferred route, along the River Nene (Old Course) through March. Accessible from either the footpath at Reed Fen Farm or from the B1099, is Dunham's Wood. Situated off the Rodham Road, this is a 2ha woodland with a wide variety of trees, guided walks, sculptures and a 20cm gauge miniature railway ☏ 01354 652134 for opening times.

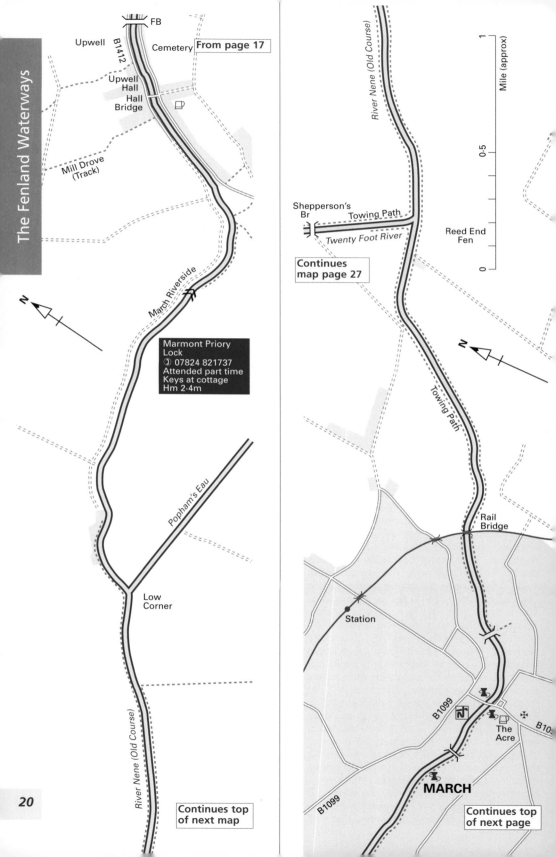

The Fenland Waterways

Upwell

Cemetery

From page 17

B1412

FB

Upwell
Hall

Hall
Bridge

Mill Drove
(Track)

March Riverside

N

Marmont Priory
Lock
☎ 07824 821737
Attended part time
Keys at cottage
Hm 2·4m

Popham's Eau

Low
Corner

River Nene (Old Course)

20

Continues top
of next map

River Nene (Old Course)

Shepperson's
Br

Towing Path

Twenty Foot River

Reed End
Fen

Continues
map page 27

Mile (approx)

1

0.5

0

N

Towing Path

Rail
Bridge

Station

B1099

The
Acre

B1099

B10

MARCH

Continues top
of next page

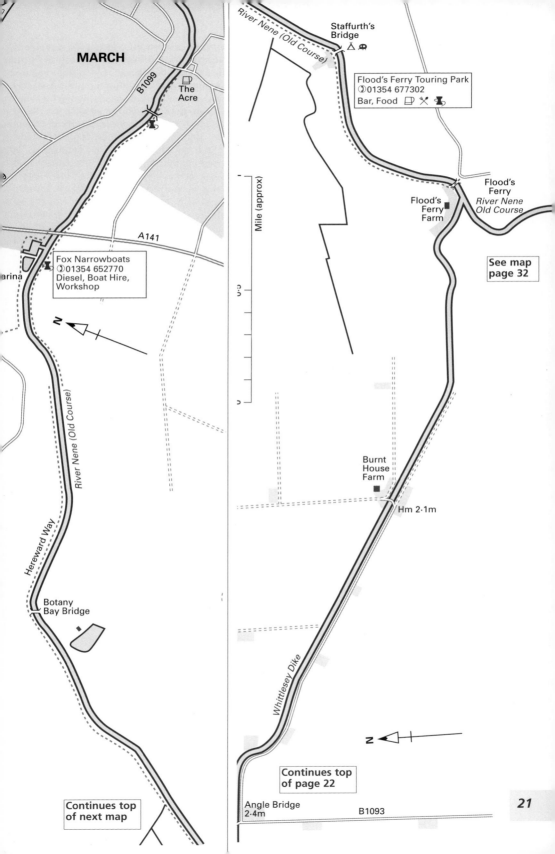

MARCH

B1099

The Acre

Flood's Ferry Touring Park
①01354 677302
Bar, Food

Staffurth's Bridge

River Nene (Old Course)

A141

Fox Narrowboats
①01354 652770
Diesel, Boat Hire,
Workshop

Marina

Flood's
Ferry
Farm

Flood's
Ferry
*River Nene
Old Course*

See map
page 32

Mile (approx)

N

River Nene (Old Course)

Hereward Way

Burnt
House
Farm

Hm 2·1m

Botany
Bay Bridge

Whittlesey Dike

N

Continues top
of page 22

Continues top
of next map

Angle Bridge
2·4m

B1093

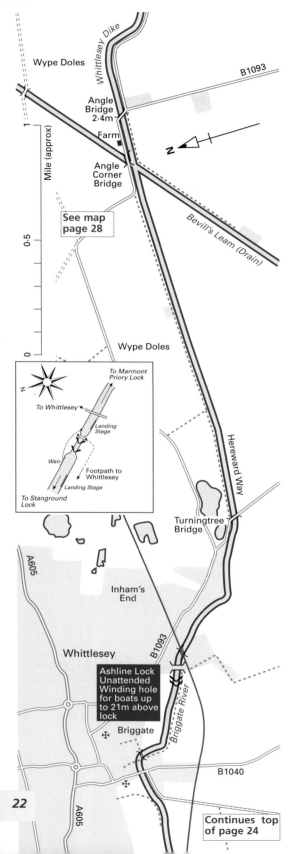

The present town of March, (Mercheford) lies midway between its Roman and Medieval predecessors. Its name means 'boundary' and all the possible boundaries to which that could relate probably derive from its position on the northern edge of a fenland isle around which the ancient River Nene flowed and beyond which open fenland stretched to the sea. This boundary is mirrored in the Roman Fen Causeway and there is much evidence of Roman settlements between Grandford House, Westry House, Estover Farm (both of whose histories can be traced to the early 13th century) and Flaggrass Hall Farm. Indeed it may have been Romans from these settlements who diverted the River Nene from its ancient northerly course southwards to what is now called the River Nene (Old Course).

After the Roman Occupation, whilst their settlements declined another, some 3km to the south, grew and by Domesday, a small hamlet of about 50 people was recorded. Although this was about 1·5km from the newly diverted river, it gradually grew over the next 200 years and became established as a trading port and small market town. It remained as such into the 16th century when there was a market and two fairs. The first church in March was a chapel to a mother church at Doddington and, as an outlying Grange to Ely it was again at the 'boundary'.

The arrival of the railway between Ely and Peterborough and between St Ives, Wisbech and Spalding in 1847/8 brought about a dramatic change. Although the port was to continue in use until the early 1900s, March was now at the centre of a railway network linking the Midlands and the North (coal and heavy industry) with East Anglia (agriculture). It rapidly developed on land to the north of the river into a large railway town and had the largest mechanised marshalling yard in the country, Whitemoor, with more than 100km of track and sidings. Over 2000 jobs were created and March became a dormitory town for railway workers.

Inevitably the railways influenced pub names (e.g. the Great Northern), street names (e.g. Locomotive Street) and the architecture. The Victorian Gothic station is decorated with curly cast-iron brackets with leaf and rosette ornaments and there are cast-iron porches such as those in Station Road and a cast-iron fountain in Broad Street commemorates the coronation of George V in 1911. Such was the importance of March that when the Isle of Ely was an administrative county, March itself was the county town.

Continues top of page 24

Despite its long history, March is somewhat of a disappointment today. There are of course exceptions and St Wendreda's Church (1·5km south of the river at Town End) is one. Standing behind chestnut trees, dedicated to a Saxon saint and dating from the early 14th century it has one of the finest church roofs in the country; a glorious double hammerbeam roof decorated with four tiers of 118 angels with outstretched wings. The church itself, mainly decorated and perpendicular, was partially rebuilt in 1528 and restored in the late 1870s. The tower, through which there is an ancient right of way, dates from the middle of the 14th century. Inside are two brasses, one somewhat worn (1501) is of William Dredeman, believed to be the donor of the roof, and his wife Joan; the other (1517) is of Anthony Hansard, his wife Katherine and their daughter. They are represented as kneeling figures in heraldic dress and the brass is decorated with their shield, scrolls, a vase of lillies and an Annunciation of the Madonna kneeling at a desk in front of the Archangel Gabriel. There are a number of amusing grotesque faces, the best being on the outside south-facing fabric.

It is said that when the people of March started to build a church, the Devil, claiming the Fens as his own, pulled down each night everything which had been made. A cross was built which successfully drove the Devil away: the remains of a 14th-century wayside cross can be seen today on the west side of the road between the church and the river.

As it passes through March, the River Nene (Old Course) lies in a deep channel with steep banks and becomes progressively narrower towards the Town Bridge. Generally there are houses on the north bank with private riverside gardens, moorings and an interesting variety of boats. There are short-stay moorings immediately east of the Town Bridge on the north bank below the thatched Ship Inn (meals). A red-brick late Victorian Town Hall (information), whose high, green copper bell tower is a prominent landmark, is on the south bank and faces a market square (market day Wednesday) and a former coaching inn, The Olde Griffin Hotel. Other inns within reach of the river include the Acre, the Red Lion and the George and there is a wide choice of restaurants and 'takeaways'. The road leads south past the Museum, housed in a former 19th-century girls' school (open Wednesday morning and Saturday ☏ 01354 653714), St Peter's Parish Church and the former Court House, to Town End and St Wendreda's Church. Immediately west of the bridge are

further moorings although the toilets and pump-out facilities are presently closed and on the north bank, a fine Georgian house is home to the Royal British Legion. Another thatched inn, the White Horse stood also on the north bank just to the west of a footbridge but is now private property and close by is a small riverside garden with Shetland ponies belonging to the 17th-century Old Brew House (accommodation).

The Hereward Way, on the south bank, passes through parkland and open countryside with bankside hawthorn trees, before crossing the river on the busy A141 March bypass to skirt Fox Narrowboats (hire-boats, boat building, workshops, moorings, diesel, pump-out, gifts, ☏ 01354 652770) on the north bank, immediately adjoining the offices and depot of the Middle Level Commissioners. After a short detour around MBM potato processing plant, the Way continues on the north bank as far as Top Hake's Farm, after which it goes inland to Turves then back along the Twenty Foot River to join Whittlesey Dyke at Angle Bridge. Although other riverside footpaths are shown on the Ordnance Survey maps, they are often little used and frequently impassable.

The river becomes progressively wider again to the west of March and flows generally within steep high banks through open fenland, under a farm access bridge near Botany Bay and past Top Hake's Farm to Staffurth's Bridge, slightly narrower to the east but wider again to the west. Here, Flood's Ferry Touring Park includes the provision of moorings, a slipway, fishing stages for disabled, a bar with snacks etc. Flood's Ferry itself, where there is a farm access bridge, is about 1·5km southwest from Staffurth's Bridge and the river is crossed here by the Greenwich Meridian Line. Guarded by a pillbox, the River Nene (Old Course), turns south towards Benwick and the route to Whittlesey continues generally westwards along Whittlesey Dyke. After a few bends, the Dyke flows northwest for about 2·5km in a straight channel past a number of farms and under Burnthouse Bridge to reach, after a long 'S' bend, Angle Bridge and Angle Corner.

At Angle Bridge, Whittlesey Dyke is crossed by Bevill's Leam (lying in a wide, straight embanked channel to the southwest, navigable as far as Bevill's Leam pumping station but providing no through route) and its extension, the Twenty Foot River (lying in a wide, straight embanked channel to the northeast, navigable as the alternative route from the River Nene (Old Course), north of March). The Dyke continues west through open fenland, past farms and a pillbox, in a straight, steep-sided channel which becomes narrower with hawthorn trees on the north bank as it approaches Turningtree Bridge. Passing another pillbox, it changes its name to the Briggate River and flows between light industry and a sewage works, under a railway and road bridge to Ashline Lock.

Ashline Lock to Stanground Lock

Immediately upstream from Ashline Lock (unattended) but where the standard key will be required for access, on the north bank, there is a winding hole for boats up to 21m in length and a length of short-stay moorings. These moorings, known locally as the Manor Leisure Centre moorings are currently due for refurbishment. After a bend to the north by yet another pillbox, the river, lying in a deep tree-lined channel, becomes very narrow indeed and just upstream from a footbridge there is a 90° bend which can be very difficult for longer vessels to navigate. The channel continues to be very narrow as it flows through Briggate on the outskirts of Whittlesey.

The Boat Inn is on the south bank, whilst on the north bank, the Hero of Aliwall public house is named after Lt Gen Sir Harry Smith. Born in 1788 in Aliwall House in St Mary's Street, Harry Smith won a decisive victory at the Battle of Aliwall (1846), the third battle of the Sikh-British War, for which he was knighted. He later became Governor of the Cape of Good Hope and died in 1860. The road continues north past the Letter 'B' free house, opposite St Andrew's Church, into Whittlesey.

Formerly Witelsig or Witsie, after a Saxon landowner Witel, Whittlesey is another ancient fenland isle town and like March lies between the river and the Roman fen causeway. Historically it is linked with Ely with Bishop Morton's Leam passing just to the north; for the benefits the leam provided, Whittlesey was taxed by the Bishops of Ely and the income used for the upkeep of Aldreth Causeway across the Old West River. Whittlesey Washes, between Morton's Leam and the River Nene are well known for skating and in the 18th century a local blacksmith made skates which were to become the famous Whittlesey Runners and which were commonly used until the late 19th century. Whilst much of Whittlesey today, with its red-yellow brick houses, pubs, shops and non-conformist chapels is the legacy of an extensive brick industry which stretched west towards Peterborough, Old Whittlesey has some appeal.

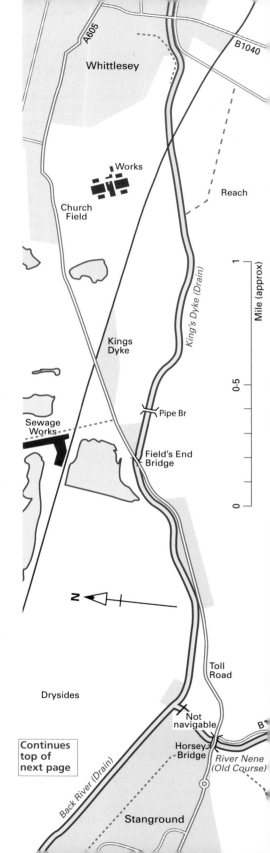

Continues top of next page

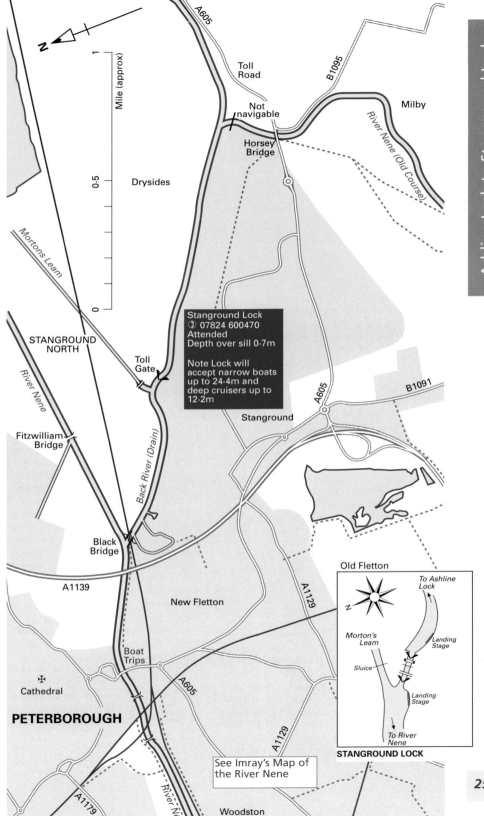

N

Mile (approx)

1

0.5

0

A605

Toll
Road

B1095

Not
navigable

Milby

Horsey
Bridge

River Nene (Old Course)

Drysides

Mortons Leam

STANGROUND
NORTH

Toll
Gate

Stanground Lock
☎ 07824 600470
Attended
Depth over sill 0·7m

Note Lock will
accept narrow boats
up to 24·4m and
deep cruisers up to
12·2m

A605

B1091

River Nene

Fitzwilliam
Bridge

Back River (Drain)

Stanground

Black
Bridge

A1139

New Fletton

A1129

Boat
Trips

⌖
Cathedral

A605

PETERBOROUGH

A1129

Old Fletton

To Ashline
Lock

Z

Morton's
Leam

Landing
Stage

Sluice

Landing
Stage

To River
Nene

STANGROUND LOCK

See Imray's Map of
the River Nene

A1179

River Nene

Woodston

See Imray's Map of
the River Nene

Once the largest parish in Cambridgeshire, there are two parish churches, St Mary's and St Andrew's. St Mary's dates from the middle of the 13th century after a fire had destroyed the earlier church in 1244 and its mid-15th-century ornate spire and tower is one of the finest in the county. Immediately south of St Mary's, the former Manor House is mainly 17th century but with some 15th century remains and the Falcon Hotel is nearby. St Andrew's, built on the site of a 12th-century church has some 13th and 14th-century windows and a 16th-century embattled tower. In the church yards the grave headstones have been moved to the surrounding walls and, at St Andrew's, also ranked in freestanding rows facing the church.

The stone-built Harrington House (c1600), the George Inn and a three-story red-brick early Georgian former post office, overlook the market square in which there is an attractive Buttercross with a tiled roof supported by stone pillars. After the Black Death, Statutes Fairs were held here at which farm labourers vied for a year's work. Another tradition which would have taken place in the Square and which survived until the early 20th century was 'Straw Bear Dancing'. On Tuesday after Plough Monday, a man covered with straw would dance like a bear in return for money. Next to a small early Victorian Town Hall with a museum (open Friday and Sunday afternoons and Saturday mornings) is the mid-17th-century Black Bull Inn.

West from Whittlesey, the river, now called the King's Dyke after King Canute who allegedly caused it to be cut, is narrow and after a row of poplar trees and a railway bridge, is lined with reeds and flag iris. To the north are extensive brick pits; to the south is open fenland. As the high banks diminish, so the river runs through open countryside, with light industry further to the north, to the A605 at Field's End Bridge (narrow). Throughout this stretch there is a good public bridle way on the south bank.

Between Field's End Bridge and Horsey Toll, the river is bordered on the north by the busy A605. Immediately south of a farm access bridge (good distant views of Peterborough Cathedral), in a clump of trees is Horsey Hill Civil War Fort. This mid-17th-century fort was pentagonal with five bastions for cannon and inside the walls were three houses and a gatehouse. It, together with the Bullwarks at Earith, guarded the roads from Huntingdonshire across the fens. West of the bridge, the River Nene (Old

Course) or Pig Water (not navigable) joins the King's Dyke. The stretch leading to Stanground Lock is straight, open to the north but bordered on the south by a large new housing estate with a bankside footpath, as the A605 has been diverted.

Stanground village, where a Bronze Age dug-out canoe was found in 1828, was first mentioned in a land grant made by King Elfwin in 952 after which it passed to the Abbots of Thorney who were patrons of the early-14th-century church of St John the Baptist. The Lampass Cross (12th century?), once used as a footbridge across a dyke, is at the entrance to the attractive, tree-lined graveyard. Stanground is now a large suburb of Peterborough.

Moreton's Leam joins the river from the northeast above the lock and the combined rivers pass Peterborough Boating Centre (chandlery, gas, diesel ✆ 01733 566688) and the Woolpack Inn (riverside garden, moorings, meals), to flow under a railway bridge to join the River Nene.

Reed Fen Farm to Angle Bridge via the Twenty Foot River

This mid-17th-century river branches northwest from the River Nene (Old Course), around the north and west of March. For the most part it lies in a deep, steep-banked channel with long straight stretches and crossed by a number of bridges.

About 1·5km from the junction, west of Shepperson's Bridge, a minor road leads to Sovereign Quarter Horses (Parkland, Suffolk Punch horses, farming bygones, refreshments ✆ 01354 651944). Between Chainbridge and Hobb's Lot Bridge, a disused railway bridge, but still with an imposing signal gantry, marks the northern end of March's Whitemoor marshalling yards (and HMP Whitemoor). It is now part of a cycleway. West from Hobb's Lot Bridge at Goosetree Farm, the river turns southwest and runs in a straight line for 9km to join Whittlesey Dyke at Angle Bridge.

There are roads and footpaths on the north bank to Hobb's Lot Bridge and thereafter on the south bank, including another length of the Hereward Way between Duncombe's Corner and Angle Bridge.

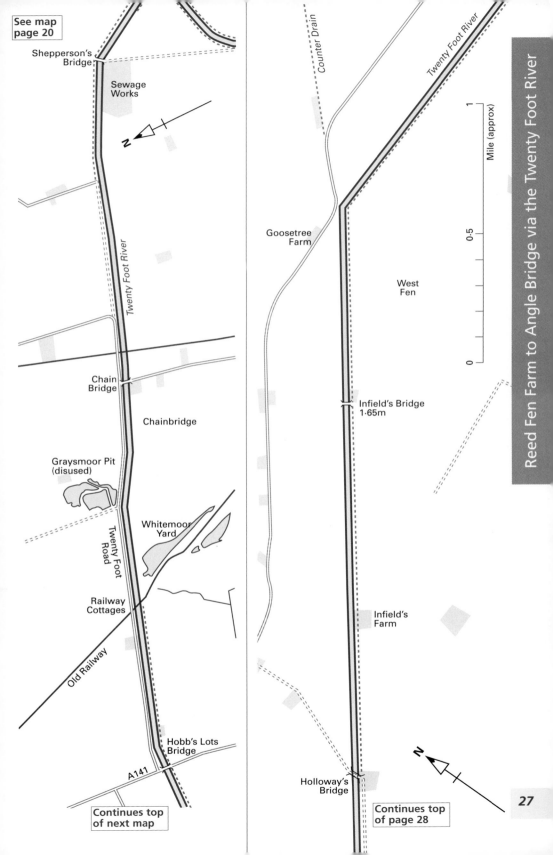

See map
page 20

Shepperson's
Bridge

Sewage
Works

N

Twenty Foot River

Chain
Bridge

Chainbridge

Graysmoor Pit
(disused)

Whitemoor
Yard

Twenty Foot Road

Railway
Cottages

Old Railway

Hobb's Lots
Bridge

A141

Continues top
of next map

Counter Drain

Twenty Foot River

Goosetree
Farm

West
Fen

1

Mile (approx)

0.5

0

Infield's Bridge
1·65m

Infield's
Farm

N

Holloway's
Bridge

Continues top
of page 28

Reed Fen Farm to Angle Bridge via the Twenty Foot River

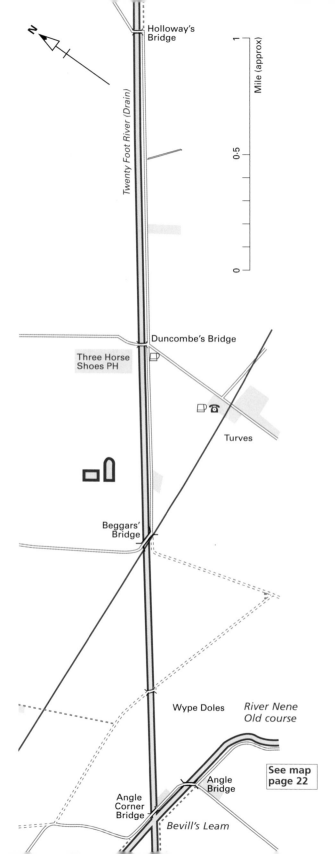

N

Holloway's
Bridge

Mile (approx)

1

0.5

0

Twenty Foot River (Drain)

Duncombe's Bridge

**Three Horse
Shoes PH**

Turves

Beggars'
Bridge

Wype Doles

*River Nene
Old course*

See map
page 22

Angle
Bridge

Angle
Corner
Bridge

Bevill's Leam

Other navigable waterways in the Middle Level

Whilst it was theoretically possible to enter the Middle Level waterways from the River Ouse via the Old Bedford Sluice, the Old Bedford River, Welches Dam Lock and Horseway Lock, the entrance at the Old Bedford Sluice is severely restricted due to heavy siltation and navigation on the Forty Foot or Vermuyden's Drain between Welches Dam Lock and Horseway Lock is closed.

The other waterways in the Middle Level can however be readily accessed from the River Nene (Old Course) at Flood's Ferry.

Flood's Ferry to Horseway Lock

West from Flood's Ferry Bridge, the River Nene (Old Course) continues along the line of its ancient channel past Ransonmoor pumping station, one of many pillboxes on this next stretch of the river, a large potato processing plant and White Fen Farm with its imposing white access bridge (and a pillbox) to Copalder Corner where it turns south to Benwick. It lies in quite a wide embanked channel and there are roads on the east and south banks.

Benwick was never a fenland isle; its houses are built on the ancient silt roddons of the River Nene, upon which the High Street now lies. There is a short attractive length of river between the B1093 road bridge and a footbridge where the river turns sharply to the northwest. The graveyard of the former St Mary's Church (1850 and built on the site of an earlier mid-17th-century chapel) is in the apex of the bend and there are plans to build a new church here. Here also are new short stay moorings, constructed by the Middle Level Commissioners for the Benwick Residents' Association and maintained by Benwick Parish Council. In the village there is a post office and stores and the Five Alls public house.

A lawyer, I plead for all;
A parson, I pray for all;
A soldier, I fight for all;
Queen Victoria, I rule all.
and underneath a workman at a plough,
I pay for all.

Leaving Benwick, the river meanders through open fenland first west under a farm access bridge by another pill box at Four Hundred Farm and then southwest after Benwick IDB pumping station. It soon leaves its ancient course and flows in a relatively straight embanked channel for about 1·5km after which it twists and turns becoming narrower for a short distance before rejoining its ancient channel again at Wells Bridge. Here the River Nene (Old Course) continues southwest to Lode's End Lock and Ramsey, whilst a sharp turn to the east leads into the Forty Foot or Vermuyden's Drain.

As its name implies, this is a wide waterway which runs between steep banks across open fenland, bordered on the north by the B1096, in an almost unbroken straight line for 8·5km to the Leonard Childs' Bridge north of Chatteris. On its way it flows under a road bridge at Ramsey Forty Foot near the George Inn, under a lattice access bridge and then past a few old cottages at Puddock Bridge.

After the bend at Leonard Childs' Bridge, the Drain continues, still across open fenland, in another unbroken straight line for 9km to Welches Dam. It is crossed by the busy A141 which leads south to Chatteris. Although not strictly a riverside town now, ancient watercourses ran to the north, west and south and it would probably have been connected to the Forty Foot Drain either by a waterway leading from the Drain to the northern part of the town or by a road (now a part of an industrial estate) leading from that part of the town to docks on the Forty Foot Drain close to where it is crossed by the A141. Indeed before Ireton's Way, (named after Henry Ireton, Oliver Cromwell's Deputy Governor of Ely, and now the A142) was built in 1643, there was no road between Chatteris and Ely and any traffic would have been waterborne.

There are a number of fen barrows and tumuli around Chatteris, for example to the south in Horsely Fen, to the southeast at Common Hill and to the north between the Sixteen and Forty Foot Drains at Honey Hill, earlier called Huna's Island. Huna was chaplain to St Etheldreda and Honey Farm may be built on the site of his chapel. After pilgrims experienced cures at his graveside, his body was removed to Thorney, to which the majority of Chatteris owed their allegiance.

Bronze Age, Iron Age and Saxon weapons have been found nearby and in 1824 a hoard of about 1,000 Roman coins were ploughed

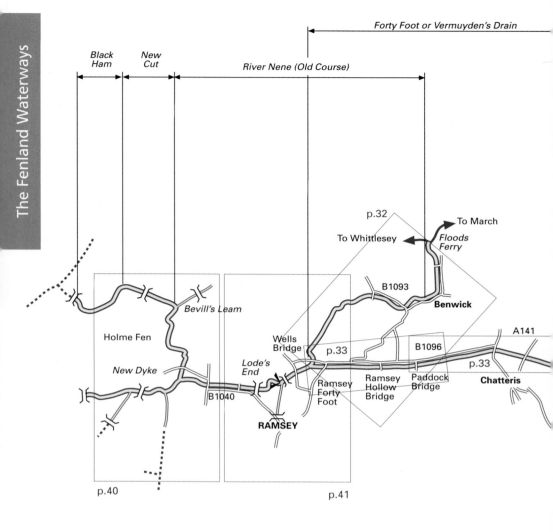

Forty Foot or Vermuyden's Drain

Black Ham

New Cut

River Nene (Old Course)

p.32

To March

To Whittlesey

Floods Ferry

B1093

Benwick

Bevill's Leam

A141

Holme Fen

Wells Bridge

p.33

B1096

New Dyke

Lode's End

Ramsey Forty Foot

Ramsey Hollow Bridge

Paddock Bridge

p.33

Chatteris

B1040

RAMSEY

p.40

p.41

RIVER OUSE TO RIVER NENE
Alternative Route

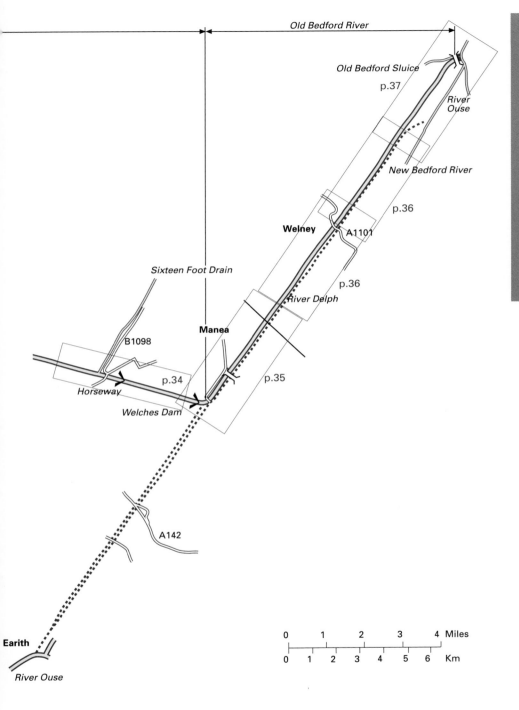

Old Bedford River

Old Bedford Sluice

p.37

River Ouse

New Bedford River

Welney A1101

p.36

Sixteen Foot Drain

p.36

River Delph

Manea

B1098

p.35

p.34

Horseway

Welches Dam

A142

0   1   2   3   4 Miles

0   1   2   3   4   5   6   Km

Earith

River Ouse

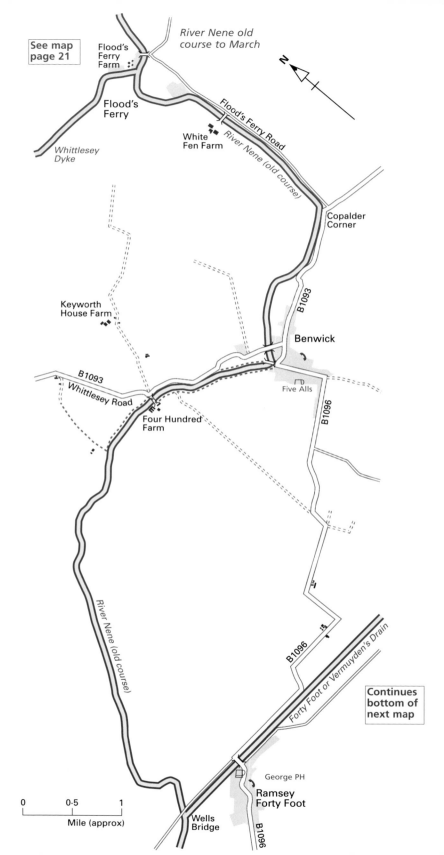

See map
page 21

Flood's
Ferry
Farm

*River Nene old
course to March*

N

Flood's
Ferry

Flood's Ferry Road

White
Fen Farm

River Nene (old course)

*Whittlesey
Dyke*

Copalder
Corner

B1093

Keyworth
House Farm

Benwick

B1093

Whittlesey Road

Five Alls

Four Hundred
Farm

B1096

River Nene (old course)

B1096

Forty Foot or Vermuyden's Drain

Continues
bottom of
next map

George PH

Ramsey
Forty Foot

0   0.5   1

Mile (approx)

Wells
Bridge

B1096

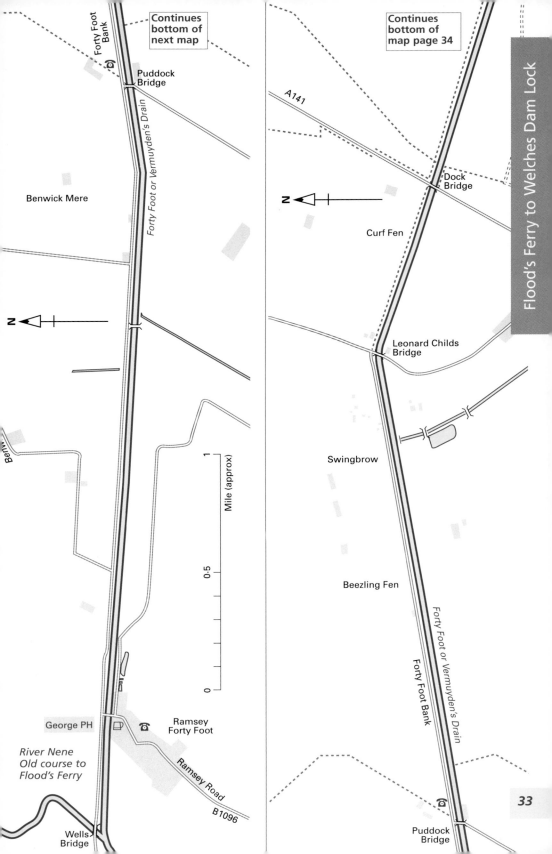

Forty Foot Bank

Continues bottom of next map

Puddock Bridge

Forty Foot or Vermuyden's Drain

Benwick Mere

N

Continues bottom of map page 34

A141

Dock Bridge

Curf Fen

N

Leonard Childs Bridge

Swingbrow

Beezling Fen

Forty Foot or Vermuyden's Drain

Forty Foot Bank

Puddock Bridge

Mile (approx)

1

0.5

0

George PH

Ramsey Forty Foot

River Nene Old course to Flood's Ferry

Ramsey Road

B1096

Wells Bridge

Benw

33

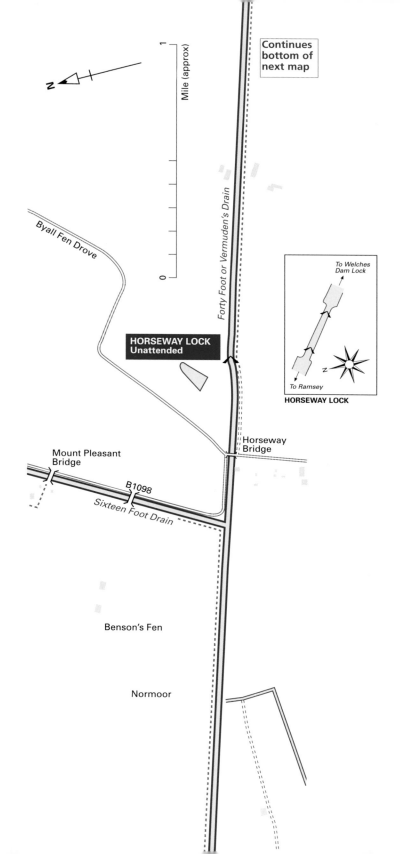

Mile (approx)

1

0

Continues
bottom of
next map

Byall Fen Drove

Forty Foot or Vermuden's Drain

**HORSEWAY LOCK
Unattended**

To Welches
Dam Lock

To Ramsey

HORSEWAY LOCK

Horseway
Bridge

Mount Pleasant
Bridge

B1098

Sixteen Foot Drain

Benson's Fen

Normoor

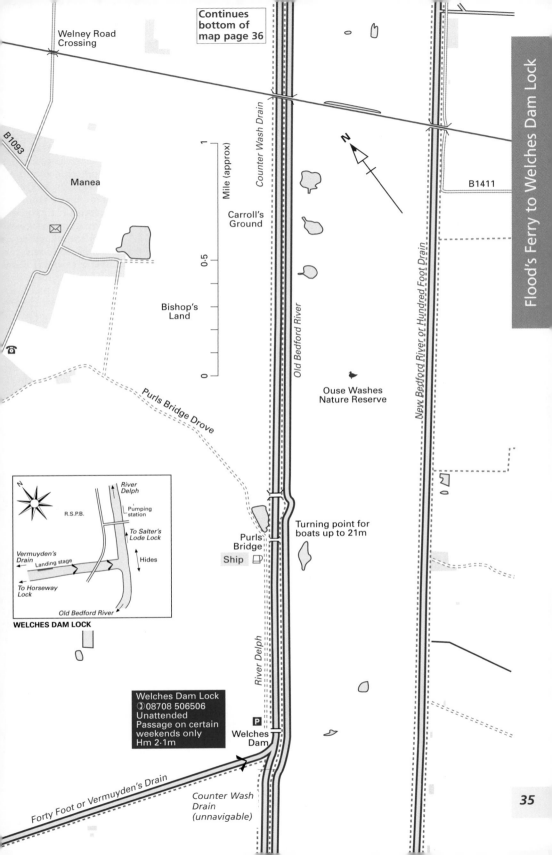

Welney Road Crossing

Continues bottom of map page 36

B1093

Manea

✉

Counter Wash Drain

Mile (approx)

1

0.5

0

Carroll's Ground

Bishop's Land

☎

Purls Bridge Drove

N

B1411

Old Bedford River

New Bedford River or Hundred Foot Drain

Ouse Washes Nature Reserve

Turning point for boats up to 21m

Purls Bridge

Ship 🛏

River Delph

WELCHES DAM LOCK

N

River Delph

Pumping station

R.S.P.B.

To Salter's Lode Lock

Vermuyden's Drain

Landing stage

Hides

To Horseway Lock

Old Bedford River

Welches Dam Lock
① 08708 506506
Unattended
Passage on certain
weekends only
Hm 2·1m

P
Welches Dam

Forty Foot or Vermuyden's Drain

Counter Wash Drain (unnavigable)

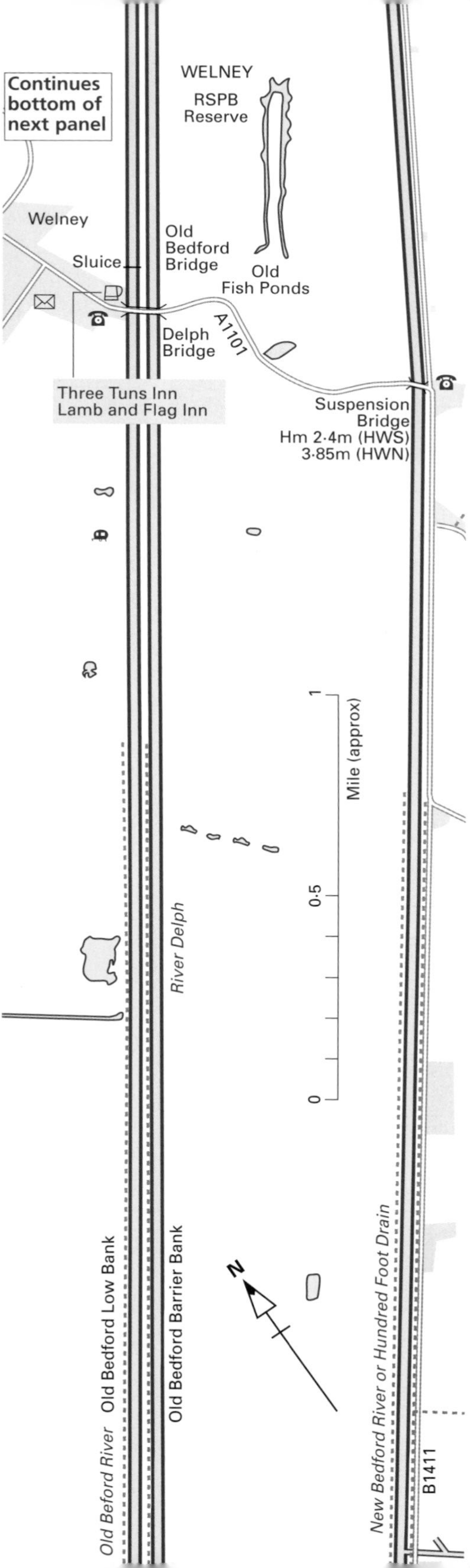

WELNEY
RSPB Reserve

Continues bottom of next panel

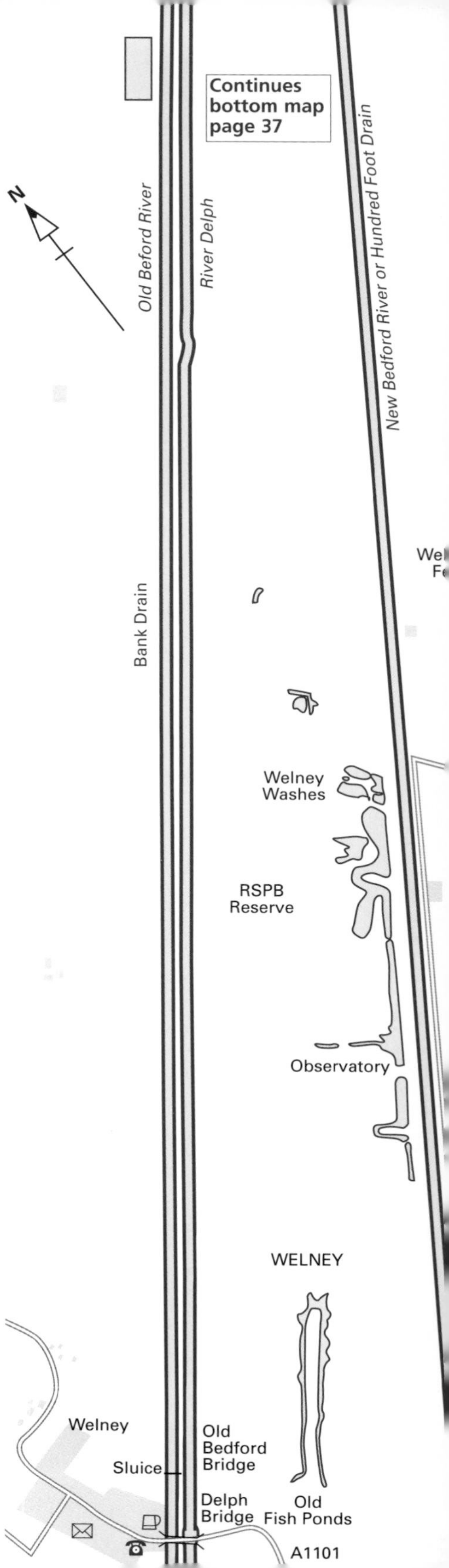

Continues bottom map page 37

Welney

Old Bedford Bridge

Sluice

Old Fish Ponds

Delph Bridge

A1101

Three Tuns Inn
Lamb and Flag Inn

Suspension Bridge
Hm 2·4m (HWS)
3·85m (HWN)

N

Old Beford River

River Delph

New Bedford River or Hundred Foot Drain

Bank Drain

Mile (approx)

1

0·5

0

River Delph

Welney Washes

RSPB Reserve

Observatory

Wel Fe

Old Bedford River   Old Bedford Low Bank

Old Bedford Barrier Bank

New Bedford River or Hundred Foot Drain

B1411

N

WELNEY

Welney

Sluice

Old Bedford Bridge

Delph Bridge

Old Fish Ponds

A1101

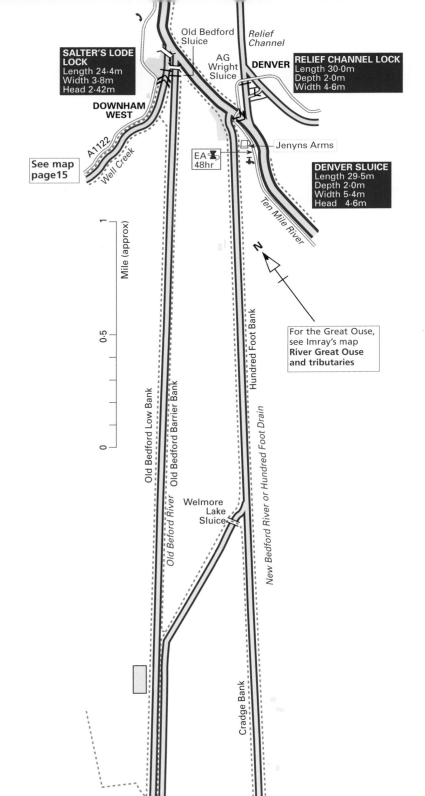

SALTER'S LODE LOCK
Length 24·4m
Width 3·8m
Head 2·42m

Old Bedford Sluice

AG Wright Sluice

Relief Channel

DENVER

RELIEF CHANNEL LOCK
Length 30·0m
Depth 2·0m
Width 4·6m

DOWNHAM WEST

A1122

Well Creek

See map page 15

EA 48hr

Jenyns Arms

DENVER SLUICE
Length 29·5m
Depth 2·0m
Width 5·4m
Head 4·6m

Ten Mile River

N

For the Great Ouse, see Imray's map **River Great Ouse and tributaries**

Mile (approx)

1

0·5

0

Old Bedford Low Bank

Old Bedford Barrier Bank

Old Bedford River

Hundred Foot Bank

New Bedford River or Hundred Foot Drain

Welmore Lake Sluice

Cradge Bank

up. Known as Cetriz, Aroysia de Clare founded a convent for Benedictine nuns here in 988, which initially belonged to Ramsey and subsequently Ely. By the Dissolution of the Monasteries there was an Abbess, a Prioress and nine nuns. Other than a few traces of the convent's walls in East and South Park Street, there are no other remains.

The parish Church of St Peter and St Paul is mainly early 20th century, however parts of the nave and the west tower are 14th century possibly having survived a fire in 1310. There are a few 18th and 19th-century houses in Market Hill and the High Street, and whilst there used to be more than 60 pubs, the few today include the Crosss Keys Hotel and the George Hotel.

3km east of the A141 road bridge, the Sixteen Foot Drain branches off northeast to Three Holes back to the River Nene (Old Course) at Upwell via Popham's Eau (see Salter's Lode Lock to Marmont Priory Lock). The Forty Foot Drain now becomes appreciably narrower and overgrown as it passes under the B1098 road bridge to Horseway Lock (unattended). Horseway lock is, however, currently closed, due to the closure of Welches Dam lock and there is currently no passage for vessels along the Forty Foot Drain east of Horseway lock. There is therefore no access to and from the Old Bedford River at this point. The route to Welches Dam can however be followed on a good farm access road and footpath on the south bank.

At Welches Dam there is a bend in the otherwise straight watercourse and bank and the rivers change their names. Although the events leading to the formation of this bend are not fully documented, they can be surmised. Vermuyden's Drain was cut in 1651 to drain water from a large area of fenland north of Chatteris and to discharge it into the Old Bedford River which had been cut some twenty years earlier. It is likely that soon after these waterways had been joined, it was realised that water introduced from Vermuyden's Drain could flow back along the Old Bedford River towards Earith instead of flowing down to Denver, causing increased upstream flooding. To prevent this a dam was built by Edmund Welche, an engineer working for Vermuyden, across the Old Bedford River just upstream of its junction with Vermuyden's Drain. Whilst water from the Cranbrook flowed around the dam into Vermuyden's Drain and thence into the lower portion of the Old Bedford River (see 3. on diagram opposite), water coming downthe

Old Bedford River, from Earith and beyond, had nowhere to go except spill into the Washes. As this second stage of Vermuyden's works had been designed to achieve year-round farming, the upstream length of the Old Bedford River was extended after a bend into a new river, the River Delph, which ran northeast parallel to the Old Bedford River to outfall eventually into the New Bedford River at Welmore Lake Sluice. At the same time a flood bank was built between the Old Bedford River and the River Delph, not only to keep the two rivers apart but also to maintain the integrity of the Washes.

As well as the lock, there are a few cottages, a large pumping station which lifts water from the surrounding rivers and fens through the Old Bedford Barrier Bank into the River Delph and the Ouse Washes Nature Reserve. This reserve, stretching for over 5km from south of Welches Dam to the railway bridge at Manea and beyond, covers some 1,000ha of wet grassland and over 75km of managed ditches lying in the Washes between the River Delph and the New Bedford River. Hides on the Old Bedford Barrier Bank are accessed from the visitors centre opposite Welches Dam Pumping Station by a bridge over the Old Bedford River (car park, toilets, hides, wheelchair access, ☎ 01354 680212).

The Old Bedford River continues northeast in a straight line with the high Middle Level Barrier Bank, the River Delph and the Washes to the east and the much lower Old Bedford Low Bank on the west which gives way to open fenland. At Purls Bridge, where there were once three pubs, there are a few houses and the riverside Ship Inn (meals). The minor road from Welches Dam leaves the riverside at Purls Bridge for Manea, an 'Island Common' where there are stores, a post office, restaurants and the Rose and Crown Inn.

King Charles had plans for building a model township at Manea to be called Charlemont and which was to be linked by a navigable waterway to the River Ouse; his plans were interrupted by the Civil War and never completed. There were to be other unsuccessful plans for Manea. North of Manea towards Welney the self-supporting Manea Colony or Cambridgeshire Community No. 1 was founded in 1838. Following the principles of Robert Owen, the social reformer and founder of the Co-Op movement, some 60ha was farmed by Colonists, motto 'Each for All', whose uniform was green tunics, trousers, straw hats or caps for men and tunics for women. Within a few years however it had run into trouble and it was abandoned in 1851.

3km northeast from Purls Bridge, the Old Bedford River is crossed by the Ely to Peterborough railway, where, it is said, the land is so flat that the earth's curvature can be seen by looking along the lines. The river continues its straight course still bordered on the east by the high Middle Level Barrier Bank, the River Delph and the Washes and the lower Old Bedford Low Bank and open fenland to the west, to Welney. There are footpaths on both banks.

Welney, on the Old Wellenhe, the Welle Stream or the Old Croft River to Upwell and Outwell, was the home of famous mid-19th century fen skaters such as 'Turkey' Smart, 'Fish' Smart and 'Gutta Percha' See, (so nicknamed for his toughness). 'Turkey' was overall Fen Champion for ten years and he is said to have put his winnings 'safely in the bank' ... he had buried them in the banks of the Old Bedford River! The Three Tuns Inn is on the river bank (free moorings for patrons) and in the village there is a post office and stores and the Lamb and Flag.

Welney is perhaps best known for the Welney Wildfowl and Wetlands Trust. Occupying some 400ha of traditionally managed washland, it is known for its wild flowers, rushes, reeds, butterflies, and dragonflies and above all for its birds, particularly during the winter when thousands of wintering wildfowl make it one of the greatest wildlife attractions in Europe. As it is on the east bank of the New Bedford River, it is accessible from Welney only by the A1101 road bridge and a minor road to the east of the New Bedford Bank. There are many hides and footpaths, an information centre, shop, tea room and parking ✆ 01353 860711.

There is a control sluice on the Old Bedford River at Welney (for operation ✆ 08708 506506). The river continues for another 9·5km, with footpaths on the flood banks, to the Old Bedford Sluice and the River Ouse at Salter's Lode. The sluice is not built in the form of a traditional lock and can only be navigated when water levels are the same on each side ✆ 01366 382292.

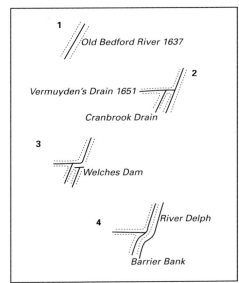

WELCHES DAM

Wells Bridge to Holme Fen

From Wells Bridge travelling west, although there are navigable waterways, there is no through navigable route. Whilst there are low bridges and some of the waterways are shallow and narrow, some say that these waters are the best to navigate (more suited to narrowboats as opposed to river cruisers). Much of the waterside land is private, with private access roads and bridges; there are few public footpaths. Perhaps because of the limited accessibility this part of Fenland is indefinably different to the more northerly fens. Although extensively farmed, there are trees, woods and remains of old windmills. It may be more like fenland used to be.

The River Nene (Old Course), now back in its old embanked channel, continues southwest under Bodsey Farm Bridge, south of which is Bodsey House on a small island dating from Saxon times and once belonging to Ramsey Abbey, through open fenland and under Saunder's Bridge, which now joins the two halves of Ramsey Golf Course, to its junction with High Lode, which leads south to Ramsey and Lode's End Lock.

High Lode initially passes through open fenland which shortly after Bill Fen Marina on the west bank (moorings, slipway, diesel, pump-out, ✆ 01487 813621) gives way to scrap industry on the west and light industry on the east. However once in Ramsey, there

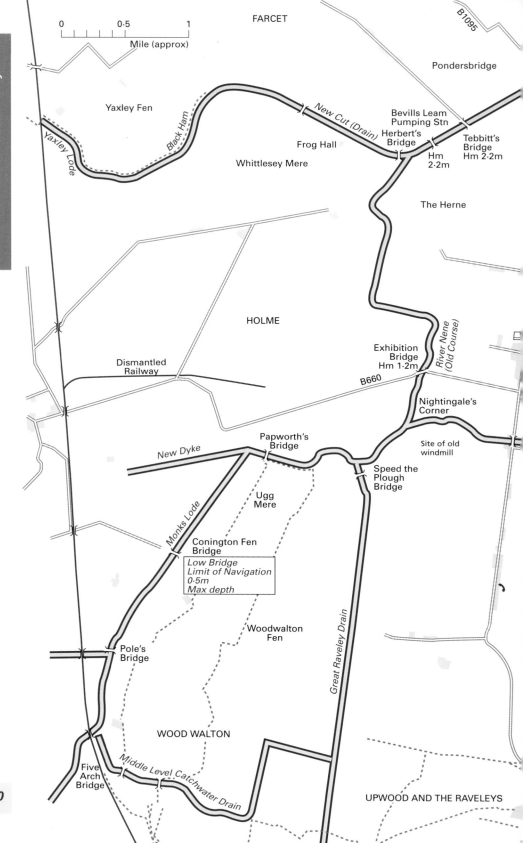

FARCET

B1095

Pondersbridge

0   0·5   1
Mile (approx)

Yaxley Fen

Yaxley Lode

Black Ham

New Cut (Drain)

Bevills Leam
Pumping Stn

Herbert's
Bridge
Hm
2·2m

Tebbitt's
Bridge
Hm 2·2m

Frog Hall

Whittlesey Mere

The Herne

HOLME

Dismantled
Railway

Exhibition
Bridge
Hm 1·2m

River Nene (Old Course)

B660

Nightingale's
Corner

New Dyke

Papworth's
Bridge

Site of old
windmill

Monks Lode

Ugg
Mere

Speed the
Plough
Bridge

Conington Fen
Bridge

Low Bridge
Limit of Navigation
0·5m
Max depth

Woodwalton
Fen

Great Raveley Drain

Pole's
Bridge

WOOD WALTON

Five
Arch
Bridge

Middle Level Catchwater Drain

UPWOOD AND THE RAVELEYS

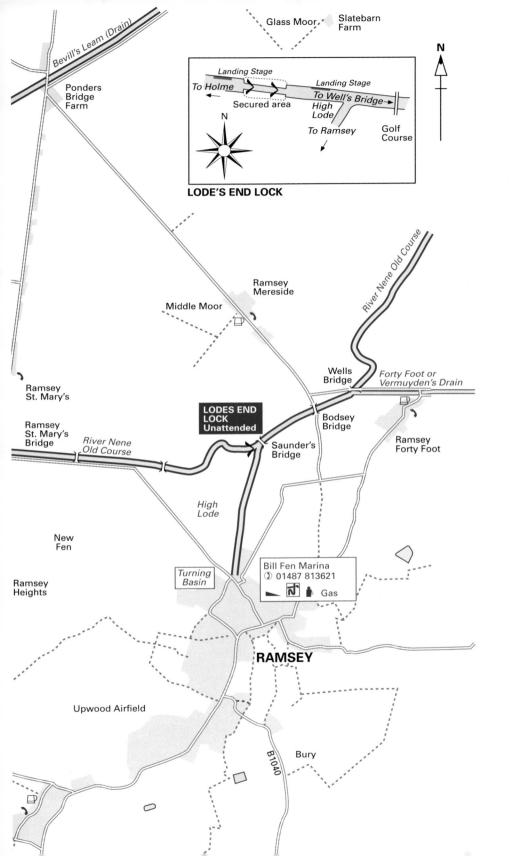

Glass Moor
Slatebarn Farm

LODE'S END LOCK

Landing Stage
To Holme
Secured area
Landing Stage
To Well's Bridge
High Lode
To Ramsey
Golf Course

N

Bevill's Leam (Drain)

Ponders Bridge Farm

River Nene Old Course

Ramsey Mereside

Middle Moor

Wells Bridge

Forty Foot or Vermuyden's Drain

Ramsey St. Mary's

Ramsey St. Mary's Bridge

River Nene Old Course

LODES END LOCK Unattended

Saunder's Bridge

Bodsey Bridge

Ramsey Forty Foot

New Fen

High Lode

Ramsey Heights

Turning Basin

Bill Fen Marina
① 01487 813621
N̂   Gas

RAMSEY

Upwood Airfield

B1040

Bury

is a well-kept area below a converted mill with a turning point but at present no public moorings.

Whilst there is evidence of nearby Bronze Age settlements, Ramsey first came to prominence in about 970 when Ramsey Abbey was founded by Aethelwine or Ailwyn, Earldorman of East Anglia. With the help of Monk Abbo from the Benedictine Abbey of Fleury on the Loire, Ramsey prospered academically, became one of the wealthiest foundations in England and the biggest landowner in Huntingdonshire, except for a short period when Geoffrey de Mandville, Earl of Essex, occupied the abbey in 1143 and turned it into a fortress. Geoffrey was killed a year later, his son returned the abbey to the monks and it continued to flourish until its dissolution in 1539. Little now remains except for some medieval masonry in the walls of the Abbey School (1652), the Parish Church of St Thomas à Beckett, parts of which were a hospital or guesthouse of the abbey and which became the Parish Church in 1875 and the remains of a 15th-century gatehouse. Now belonging to the National Trust (open daily April to October), a large part of the gate was removed by the Cromwell family to Hinchingbrooke House. Immediately inside is a somewhat startling bearded effigy probably of Ailwyn, or possibly of a Saxon Prince. In front of the gatehouse and the abbey grounds (open Sunday afternoons) are attractive greens with a pond surrounded by almshouses.

In the meantime a small town and port became established along the small river which ran down the middle of the Great Whyte; it was covered over in 1853/4. The town received the grant of a market in 1200 and a fair in 1267. By the mid-18th century, the market had become one of the best in England for cattle and wildfowl. Many of the old buildings were destroyed by a series of fires and the town had lost much of its prominence by the 19th century. Further damage occurred in 1940 when a bomber dropped its whole load of bombs on the town.

In the town today are shops, banks, a supermarket near the river, 'takeaways' and inns include the Railway, the Jolly Sailor, the Angel, the Three Horseshoes and the George.

After Lode's End Lock, the main river meanders in its old course for about 1·5km, passing to the south, a single electricity-generating windmill, to Green Hall Farm access bridge after which it flows through a straight artificial stretch, under Bank Farm access bridge, and bordered on the south by the B1040, to the road bridge at Ramsey St Mary. Entering fairly remote and relatively inaccessible fenland, it flows past a ruined windmill on the north bank and a small clump of trees on slightly higher ground to the south (perhaps the site of an early bank burst), round what would have formed the northern edge of the ancient Ugg Mere to Nightingale's Corner. This was at the northwest corner of the old Mere where the river had originally entered it from the north. Draining the Mere and maintaining the river round its northern perimeter resulted in the sharp bend at Nightingale's Corner. Here the river divides, encompassing Holme Fen, one branch turning southwest past the former crossing of the Holme to Ramsey Railway (1863–1973) to Woodwalton and Connington Fens, the other, the River Nene (Old Course), going north towards Pondersbridge and Yaxley.

Continuing southwest, the relatively wide river meanders between steep banks for about 0·5km to Speed the Plough Bridge. This low bridge crosses the Great Raveley Drain which runs south in a virtually straight embanked channel, across open fenland and past a pumping station, to Wood Walton Fen and the limit of navigation at Great Raveley Drain Control Sluice. The drain here is quite wide (c10m) and there is no turning point. Just upstream of the sluice, Jackson's Bridge (accessible by road from Ramsey Heights) leads into English Nature's Wood Walton Fen National Nature Reserve where undrained fenland is preserved in stretches of open water, reed, swamps, sedge, heath and mixed woodland. ☎ 01487 812363.

Beyond Speed the Plough and a series of bends, the principal river, the embanked New Dyke, continues west through open fenland, past farms to Papworth's Bridge, a farm access bridge leading north to the B660. Just to the west of this bridge, Monk's Lode branches off southwest. This embanked, straight, shallow and fairly narrow (c7m) channel flows between a ruined windmill and a copse of trees for about 1·5km to Connington Fen Bridge, the limit of navigation. There is no turning point.

New Dyke continues west now in a straight embanked channel, still through open fenland, for about 1·5km to Fen Farm after which the dyke becomes much shallower and narrower with weed and reed growth. It meanders past the old Top Farm house towards the East Coast Main Line railway and a turning point at the limit of navigation.

North from Nightingale's Corner, the River Nene (Old Course) proceeds in an embanked channel across open fenland, under the B660 at Stoke's Bridge, to Stoke's Farm where it turns east to Old Decoy Farm. The sudden bend at this farm is at the southern extremity of the former Whittlesey Mere. After this old mere was finally drained by pumping in 1851/2, a river (known variously as the River Nene (Old Course), New or North Western Cut, Black Ham Drain and Yaxley Lode Drain) was maintained around its eastern and northern edges towards Yaxley (similar to the situation at Ugg Mere).

After Old Decoy Farm, the river runs in a straight line for about 1km across open fenland before turning to Johnson's Point and the Holme Fen Engine Drain. A further short, straight stretch then leads to Herbert's Bridge. Here Bevill's Leam continues northeast in a very wide channel which is navigable but only for a few hundred meters as far as the barrier formed by Bevill's Leam Pumping Station. There is plenty of room for turning. (Note: The Leam is navigable beyond the pumping station, but has to be accessed from Angle Bridge Corner on the Whittlesey Dyke).

The principal watercourse now called the New or North Western Cut, turns through 300° under Herbert's Bridge (derelict) to flow above the surrounding open fenland in a straight stretch, generally unembanked but within steep banks, before curving gently around the northern and western edges of the old Whittlesey Mere. As it does so it changes its name first to Black Ham Drain and then finally to Yaxley Lode. It is this lode, now quite shallow, which leads to the limit of navigation, the East Coast Main Line railway crossing. Here the lode is about 8m wide and there is no turning point. A footpath, which had been on the northern and eastern banks of the Black Ham Drain and Yaxley Lode, crosses to the west bank at the railway bridge and follows the lode, now only about 5m wide, to reach Yaxley and the nearby Duck and Drake free house after crossing the lode once again at a small gauging station.

The waterways of the Middle Level cross some of the most intensively farmed and drained land in the country. There is however a price to pay; the fenland soils are shrinking and wasting. This can not be better illustrated than by the Holme Fen Posts in Natural England's National Nature Reserve at Holme Fen ☎ 01487 812363. This is accessible from a minor road running northeast from Holme along Holme Lode and lying between Yaxley Lode and Black Ham Lode to the north and New Dyke and Monk's Lode to the south. In c1851, when Whittlesey Mere was drained, an iron post, reputedly from the Great Exhibition and possibly replacing an earlier oak post, was driven through the peat into the underlying firm clay and the top of the post was made level with the ground, thus providing a permanent measuring stick. By 1957 the level of the surrounding land had dropped by about 3·5m and to measure future shrinkage, a second post was placed on a reinforced concrete pile which had been driven into the clay about 6m from the first post.

The Fens; past, present and future

The beginning

Between 100 and 70 million years ago, during the early Cretaceous period, the North Sea extended across much of East Anglia and North West Europe and in this vast basin deposits of clay and chalk were laid down on underlying Jurassic clays. Further chalk deposition probably took place during the late Cretaceous period 70 to 40 million years ago. Then as a result of earth movements all these deposits were gradually raised well above sea level to form a huge landmass joining the whole of East Anglia with North West Europe and across which the predecessors of the East Anglian rivers and the Thames and the Rhine flowed east and north. There followed a long period during which these rivers gradually eroded the chalk away to form great river basins, of which the Wash is a remnant, to expose once again the Jurassic clays and to create in them a slightly undulating landscape with scattered outliers of less resistant rocks which would later form the fenland 'islands'.

During the later part of the Pleistocene period, some 18,000 years ago, the last great ice sheet reached its southernmost extension covering most of this region. About 8,000 years later, as the weather improved and the ice retreated, the basins emerged once again, largely unaltered except for a capping of Boulder Clay on the higher 'islands'. As the ice melted, two very significant things happened. First the sea-level rose by up to 100m and secondly East Anglia began to tilt slowly downwards. England became separated from North West Europe, the sea flooded into part of the East Anglian river basin to form the Wash and the remainder of the basin was poised to become today's Fenland.

There followed a long and complicated process of silt and clay deposition in the inland basin. To begin with the tides brought in marine silts which were deposited in the shallow waters at the seaward edge of the basin. As the deposits rose, salt marsh plants became established which in turn resulted in further silt deposition. Thus the edge of the basin became silted up and a kind of tidal 'barrier' emerged. Meanwhile the rivers brought their fresh water silts into the basin. Not only were these deposited in the river valleys but because of the barrier there were often periods of fresh water flooding and so these silts were also deposited over a very wide area. Trees and plants became established.

Although the major changes had been brought about by the melting ice caps, there were two more significant marine invasions. The first occurred between 6,000 and 4,000 years ago and a layer of silt and clay, the Barroway Beds, was deposited. This killed the underlying vegetation and so the first layers of peat were formed. However as these layers of silt and clay rose above the mean tide level so the vegetation became established again and as it decayed a second extensive layer of peat, the Nordelph Peat, was laid down. The second marine invasion occurred about 2,000 years ago and deposited yet another layer of silts and clays, the Terrington Beds, not only over much of the Barroway Beds and the northern part of the Nordelph Peat but also, since the strong tidal flow overcame the much weaker fresh water flow, along the river valleys.

Further changes were brought about because the relative level of land and sea fluctuated. Whilst in general East Anglia was slowly tilting seawards, there were periods when this process reversed. When the land was sinking, clay was deposited in the deeper waters and the tidal silts were not only deposited further inland but they were carried far up the rivers onto whose beds they were then deposited. The fresh water thus found its way to the sea, becoming increasingly choked and so it flooded, with its load of silt, over the southern fenland.

When the land was rising, the gradient to the sea became so shallow that the fresh water still could not escape easily and so it continued to flood but over a wider area. The fresh water lagoons and maze of sluggish watercourses through which the water tried to escape to the sea were ideal for the formation of marshes and plant growth which in turn as they decayed, gave rise to more peat deposits.

There were in-between periods when the land dried out and was no longer waterlogged. During the Bronze Age for example trees grew and the fens could be crossed freely and during the Roman occupation settlements spread out into the marine silt lands.

Because of the long complicated process of deposition, the boundaries between the fresh water peats and silts, the marine silts and the clay are complex with layers of one overlapping layers of another. In general however the marine silts and clays of the Terrington and Barroway Beds intrude into peaty fenland in a wedge running south from between Wisbech and Downham Market to Littleport and southeast from Thorney, round March, also to Littleport. From Littleport they have intruded even further along the old river beds towards Cambridge and Lakenheath.

Thus Fenland, a low-lying often waterlogged peaty and silty land with a myriad of watercourses, meres and swamps interspersed with a few 'islands' of dry land, gradually evolved.

Early Fenland Rivers

A very complex pattern of rivers and streams developed in the Barroway Beds and marine and fresh water silts, sands and fine gravels were deposited both on their beds and, like levees, along their banks. Although these beds and their drainage network were to become covered by the Nordelph Peat and the Terrington Beds, because the silts, sands and fine gravels were less easily compressed than the surrounding softer clays and silts, winding ridges, known as 'Roddons' or 'Rodhams' and mirroring the rivers and streams, emerged. Similar processes occurred in the Terrington Beds as the fens were drained.

These Roddons provide one of the best means of tracing the ancient rivers and despite years of weathering, drainage and agricultural working many of them are visible today either as prominent ridges standing proud of the surrounding land or as bands of lighter coloured silty, sandy soils contrasting with the much darker peat, or both. Even where they are not immediately evident, there are several ways in which they can be traced. For example, since they are made up of relatively hard consolidated materials, they have been used frequently from Roman times as foundations for cottages, houses, farms, churches, lanes, roads, villages and even modern housing estates. Thus sinuous roads or lines of houses can often reflect old river channels. Another means of tracing the Roddons is from the air; not only do the lighter coloured silts show up very clearly, particularly after ploughing, but the growth and colour of vegetation can be affected.

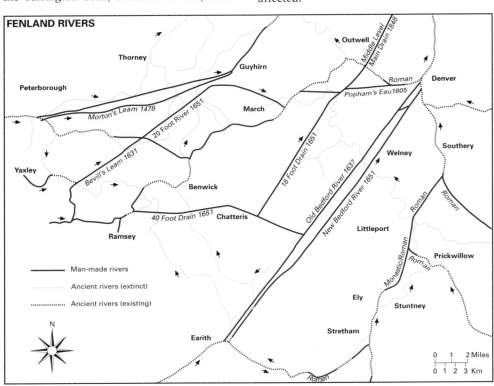

FENLAND RIVERS

Thorney · Guyhirn · Outwell · Middle Level Main Drain 1848 · Roman · Denver · Peterborough · Popham's Eau 1605 · Morton's Leam 1478 · 20 Foot River 1651 · March · Bevill's Leam 1631 · 16 Foot Drain 1651 · Old Bedford River 1637 · New Bedford River 1651 · Welney · Southery · Yaxley · Benwick · 40 Foot Drain 1651 · Chatteris · Littleport · Roman · Roman · Prickwillow · Ramsey · Monastic/Roman · Roman · Ely · Stuntney · Earith · Stretham · Roman

——— Man-made rivers
――― Ancient rivers (extinct)
··········· Ancient rivers (existing)

N

0 1 2 Miles
0 1 2 3 Km

The Fens; past, present and future

45

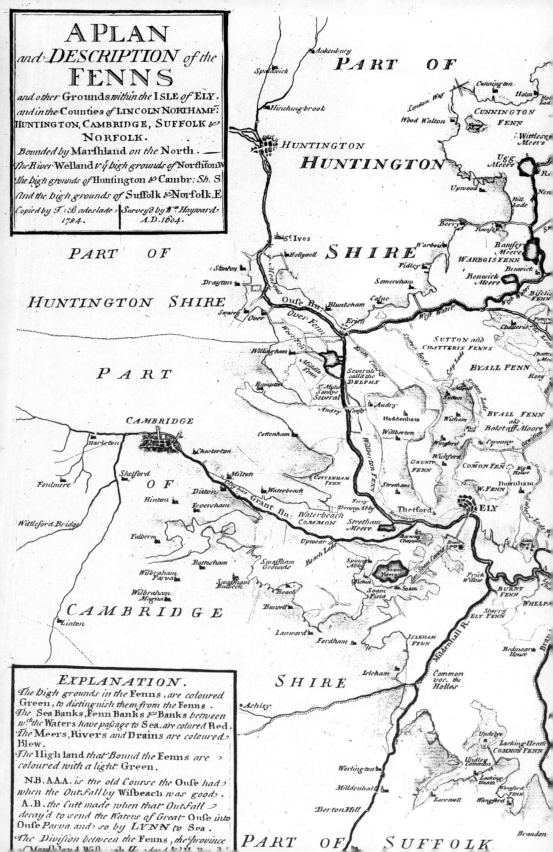

William Hayward's 'Plan and Description of the Fennes' 1604. This is reproduced courtesey of the Norris Museum, St Ives

PART · OF

HUNTINGTON

SHIRE

Oule flu:

HUNTINGTON

PART OF

CAMBRIDGE

CAMBRIDGE

SHIRE

Sautry

Wood Walton

Upwood

Berry

Warbois

Pedley

Somersham

Hollywell

St. Ives

Swavsey

Over

Over Bank

Cunington Holme

Ramsey
Tuffmoor

Bery
Fenn

Rowly
Hard

Somersham
Fenn

Somersham
Comon

Blunfham

Erith

Willingham
Fenn

Willingham

Middle
Fenn

Hermitage
Sluice

Haddenham
Fenn

Audry
Bridge

Rampton
Cottenham

Rampton
Fenn

Cotenham
Herd

Chesterton

Milton

Waterbeach

Diton

Fulbern

Botlesham

Denny
Abby

Fen to Mou

Waterbeach
joint Fenn

Upware

Waterbeach

Stretham Meere

Wicken
Fenn

Soham
Meere

Soham

Swaffham
Capa

Swaffham
Leigh Fenn

Wicken

Reech

Swaffham
Bulbeck

Swaffham
Priory

Burwell

Lanwade

Fordham

Stillton

Yarley

Standground

Wittlesey
Meere

Ugg
Meere

Ramsey
Meer

Moore
Ramsey
Meere

Ramsey

Ramsey
Hollow

Warbois
Fenn

Puttocks Drain

This Fenn did contain 100 Acres

West Water

Velwood

Chatteris

Chatteris Fenns

Mead
Land

Sutton

Mepall

Wilberton

Witchford

Stretham

Barcencer

Thetford

ELY

Downham

Great Fenn Drain

West Moor

Bedford River

New Bedford River and Bank

SOUTH

Wood Fenn

Burnt
Fenn

Ely Mow
Fenn

Comon

Wicken

Soham
Fenn

Fordham
Fenn

Isleham

Mildenhall River

Mildenhall
Mow
Fenn

Milden
Comon
Fenn

Worlington

Burton
Mill

Milldenhall
Mill

Earswell

PETERBORO

Peterboro
Little
Fenn

Eye

MIDDLE

West Fenn
Severals

West Fenn
Great

West Fenn

Flag
Fenn

Glaff

Wittlesey
Fenn

Benwick

Ranson Moor

Borrough
Moor

Common
Field

Dodington

March

LEVEL

Stony
Fenn

Manea

Norwold
Green

Eximoor

Stretham

LEVEL

Rook
Fenn

Oule flu

Whelpmoor

LEVEL

PART

OF SUFFOLK

Thomas Badeslade's 'A Mapp of the Great Level of ye Fenns', 1723. This is reproduced courtesy of the Norris Museum, St Ives

Other clues can be gained for example from examining modern administrative boundaries. Some of them date back many years and follow what were once the only natural boundaries, namely the rivers. There are historical documents dating back to the Anglo Saxons which make references to the fens and their rivers and meres. Map makers of the late-16th and early-17th century produced very detailed maps of the rivers and once adjustments have been made because of varying and various scales, their representation of many of the rivers is remarkably close to that revealed by modern geological and soil surveys. Lastly there are rivers and streams today which still follow their ancient courses.

Whilst it is difficult to separate the drainage patterns associated with the major geological events, a general picture emerges which is very different to that known today. Latter-day names are used to help understand this pattern involving three principal rivers, the Western Ouse, the Nene and the Eastern Ouse and their tributaries, all of which combined to form a delta-like maze of rivers in a flat landscape.

The Western Ouse

At Earith, the Western Ouse was joined by the Aldreth or Old West River. This tributary flowed from east to west and had risen about 3km east of Aldreth, possibly carrying water from the higher lands around Rampton, Oakington and Histon. On entering Fenland, the river flowed north for about 2km before dividing into two principal streams. One turned first east, then north under Sutton before turning northwest past Chatteris to Benwick. The other flowed generally northwest passing east of Somersham and Ramsey. Here it divided again. One channel flowed north through Benwick Mere to Benwick where it re-joined the eastern stream. The other channel flowed in a somewhat erratic manner north through Ramsey Mere, where it was joined by the River Nene. It then flowed east to Benwick where it too re-joined the eastern stream to form one large river, the River Nene, flowing east and north from Benwick to March.

At some later date the east and west streams were joined south of Chatteris, probably artificially during the Roman occupation when the Car Dyke linking Cambridge with Peterborough and Lincoln was built. Since this provided a very direct route between Earith and Benwick, the other streams were rapidly made redundant and, called the West Water, it became the principal river.

Much evidence of these rivers remains today. At Earith, the first 0·5km of the New Bedford River and then the old Huntingdonshire/Cambridgeshire county boundary follow the river's course to its first division. The northeast branch passes close to Ring Farm before it is crossed by the Bedford Rivers after which it is reflected in the twisting length of the B1381. Crossed for a second time by the Bedford Rivers, its course is then marked by a number of farms and particularly by Hammond's Eau. After Old Halves Farm its course is picked up again along a short length of the B1050 at the Crafty Fox Inn below Ferry Hill near Chatteris. For the next 7km to the B1096, the old county boundary, a bend on the A141 and the Crease Drain follow its course. North of the B1096 near Housholds Farm it is joined by one of the western branches and a track, Great Lots Road, lies on its western bank. Much of Benwick and its roads have their foundations on the river's gravels and silts.

After its first division near Earith, the Cranbrook Drain, the old county boundary and the B1050 all follow the course of the north western branch as far as a sharp bend on the B1050 at Mill Farm Cottage. The road and the county boundary then follow the straight 'artificial' link to the Crafty Fox Inn where it rejoins the northeastern branch. After Mill Farm Cottage traces of the northwestern branch become less distinct, however farms such as Lants, Red Tile, Dawsons, Marley, Warlech etc. appear to have been built on its geologically proven course.

The Nene

The River Nene entered Fenland to the east of Peterborough and appears to have divided into two principal streams. One probably flowed northeast out of the Middle Level through Flag Fen after which it too seems to have divided. One branch continued northeast towards St Vincent's Cross near Crowland, along the line of the Cat Water before turning east along the course of the Old South Eau to Cloughs Cross. Here it was joined not only by the second branch which had taken the more direct route past Thorney, but also by some waters from the combined Ouse and Nene network, before turning northwest and then north to the sea near Tydd St Mary.

The second principal stream flowed initially southeast into the Middle Level and, like the northern stream, it is likely that it divided into two. One branch flowed south into Whittlesey Mere, from which the water drained in both a fairly direct easterly route and a more round-about route through Ugg Mere and Ramsey Mere, towards Benwick, where it was joined by the Western Ouse. The combined waters then flowed north to be joined, near Flood's Ferry, by the second of the two branches which had taken a direct easterly route from Peterborough. Together, passing to the west and north of March, they then flowed to Guyhirn and the sea either directly at Wisbech or through the longer route at Tydd St Mary.

In spite of some apparently 'artificial' watercourses, for example around the edge of Whittlesey Mere, from the bridge at Ramsey St Mary along the B1040 to New Fen Farm, from Wells Bridge on the B1096 northeast to Dairy Farm and between Staffurth's Bridge and Hake's Farm, the ancient southern branch of the Nene can be traced along existing waterways. From Stanground, these are called respectively, the River Nene (Old Course), Pig Water, Yaxley Lode, Black Horse Drain and once again the River Nene (Old Course) through Benwick to Botany Bay Farm near March, where the River Nene (Old Course) leaves the ancient river to flow through March.

Benwick itself is built on the river silts and gravels as must be many farms to the north such as Flood's Ferry, Staffurth's, Ransonmoor, Top Hake's, Red House etc. and Plantwater Farm is a reminder of the Plant Water, shown on early-17th-century maps, which flowed north to Guyhirn probably along one of the ancient river beds.

The second of the two southern branches can be traced from Stanground, along part of the old A605, King's Dyke, Briggate River, parts of Whittlesey Dyke and after what is probably an artificial cut southeast of Whittlesey, along the B1093 past Angle Bridge to Bank, Cherry and Smalley's Farms. Thereafter whilst its course is more difficult to pick up, farms such as Willow, Whitemoor and Rookery may well be founded on its silts and gravels.

The Eastern Ouse and its tributaries

The River Cam flowed northeast from Cambridge towards Stretham where it was joined from the west by a tributary which was later to be linked artificially with the Aldreth or Old West River, to form the Eastern Ouse. Whilst there is some geological evidence of a watercourse at Ely, this probably flowed south for a short distance until it met the main stream which passed well to the east of Ely close to the higher lands at Stuntney. Soon after Stuntney and a series of meanders, it was joined by a major tributary (the predecessor to the River Lark), after which it gradually turned north and then northwest to Littleport where there was another major tributary (to become the Little Ouse). These combined waters continued to flow northwest past Welney, meeting further tributaries, principally the River Wissey, to Upwell where it became united with the Western Ouse and the southern part of the Nene. This important river continued through Outwell to the sea at Wisbech.

These river valleys can be traced quite easily today. The River Cam follows its ancient course northwards to Popes Corner where it is joined by the Old West River, also running in the ancient bed of the earlier tributary. Their combined waters, now often called the Ely Ouse, remain in the ancient bed as far as the point where they are crossed by the Ely to Ipswich railway line. Here the extinct river turned northeast towards Stuntney, the lighter coloured silts of its levees showing up against the darker fen peats. Between Stuntney and Prickwillow, Roll's Lode follows its course as far as the former Plough Inn, 3km east of Ely and then it lies just to the north of the Middle Fen Bank. Not only is Prickwillow built on the Eastern Ouse's levees, very similar to Benwick, but it is where it was joined by a tributary now called the River Lark which still follows its predecessor's course for about 2km downstream. Near Tom's Hole Farm, the old river turned north away from the present river, towards Littleport, its course lying just to the west of the public footpath joining Littleport with Prickwillow.

Immediately to the east of Littleport, the Eastern Ouse was joined by another tributary, now called the Little Ouse. Although this river is not strictly in the Middle Level region, its prominent Roddons running close to and criss-crossing the A1101, are amongst the best in the country. The former course of the Eastern Ouse itself can be traced along footpaths, contour lines, the Old Croft River (now a small drain), the A1101 through Welney, another stretch of the Old Croft River, the Norfolk/Cambridgeshire County boundary, the B1412 and A1122 through Upwell and Outwell, the A1101 and so to the sea at Wisbech.

Mankind's Influence

The early days

Whilst Iron Age man settled around the edge of the fens, he did not penetrate further. It was the Romans who were amongst the first to realise the potential wealth that could be gained from cultivating the fen peats and particularly the slightly higher fen silts. It was these silts which, from the 1st century, they tended to colonize and they improved both drainage and communications by building sea banks, roads and canals. The ancient sea banks which run from Wisbech eastwards towards Kings Lynn are believed to be of Roman origin. A Roman road was built from Swaffham and the Devil's Dyke to Denver and thence, lying mainly on the older silts, right across the fens to Nordelph, March, Whittlesey, Stanground and Peterborough. It passes through earthworks, possibly the remains of a Roman fort, just to the north of Christchurch between Nordelph and March.

However their most ambitious work was the building of the Car Dyke. This was a waterway, part natural and part artificial which started from the River Cam between Horningsea and Clayhythe and ran for some 110km past Earith and Benwick to Peterborough and beyond to the River Witham and Lincoln. Whilst it was probably used mainly for navigation it also served as a useful catchwater drain. Other significant works attributed to the Romans include the linking at Nordelph of the ancient tributary running east from Outwell with the small tributary of the river which ran north to the sea at King's Lynn, thus forming the Well Creek. On the eastern edge of the fenland they straightened the lower reaches of the rivers Lark and Little Ouse and at the same time might have diverted the Eastern Ouse northwards at Littleport, thus enabling it too to flow to the sea at King's Lynn.

By the 4th century however the land was going through yet another change and as the relative sea levels rose, the Romans had to embank their fields to prevent them from flooding. When they finally left Britain, their works gradually fell into disrepair and the land once again reverted to a watery waste.

The next significant period to impact on the fens was that of the monastic building starting in the middle of the 7th century. Great monasteries were founded around the edge of the fens including for example, Spalding, Peterborough (Medehamstede), Sawtry, Thetford and Bury St Edmunds. That monasteries such as Crowland, Thorney, Chatteris, Ramsey and Ely were founded within the fens may in part be due to the reputation that they were acquiring since the departure of the Romans, namely one of an evil area suffering from ague, malaria, mists, 'dark vapours', brigands and bandits, all of which were thought to be conducive to monastic life.

Many of the associated churches, abbeys and cathedrals were built from Barnack Stone, much of which would have been transported by water. Certainly there would have been an improvement in both the natural and artificial waterways and more would have been made, possibly including the joining of the two waterways which now form the Old West River. Whatever the exact date it is likely that such a complete waterway existed by the early 14th century as there is a theory that the timbers used for the construction of the Octagon Tower of Ely Cathedral were transported by water from forests near Chicksands in Bedfordshire to Ely. In a similar vein it is likely that, if not already accomplished by the Romans, both the Eastern Ouse was diverted from Stuntney to Ely and northwards from Littleport to join rivers flowing to King's Lynn and the Western Ouse diverted to flow through March and so to Upwell.

Despite their evil reputation, life in the fens was becoming established. As early as AD 656 reference is made to places, roads, streams, fens, meres, lakes, land and houses in the grant of a large area of fenland encompassed by Peterborough, Northborough, Trockenhalt, Wisbech, Benwick, Huntingdon, Whittlesey Mere and back to Peterborough made by King Wulfhere to the monastry at Peterborough. In AD 963 rights of toll over a similar area were granted, again to Peterborough, by King Edgar who also 'desired that a market be created' in King's Delph (just southwest of Whittlesey).

Draining the Fens

During the late-13th and early-14th century, as the estuary at Wisbech became clogged with silts and sands, the Nene and Western Ouse flowed increasingly along Well Creek to join the Eastern Ouse near Denver and thence to the sea at King's Lynn. However because of obstructions at Outwell, navigators could not always use this route. Instead they had to travel back along the old Eastern Ouse to Littleport and then down to

Denver and King's Lynn; a very long route. Because the problems in managing not only these rivers but also the numerous other waterways and dykes, Commissions of Sewers, the first 'Fen Conservators', were appointed and landowners were required to carry out works in proportion to the amount of land held and benefits derived. Such principles are enshrined in and are the mainstay of today's legislation.

John Morton, Bishop of Ely and Lord Chancellor of England was the first to recognise that straightening watercourses would speed up their flow. He built (1478–80) Morton's Leam, a drain 19km long by 12·2m wide and 1·2m deep, to carry the Nene from Stanground in Peterborough in a straight line to Guyhirn. Although improved and remade several times, it was Morton's Leam that set the precedent for all the major 17th-century drainage works.

The first of these was a drainage project around Upwell sponsored by the 75-year old Lord Chief Justice Sir John Popham in 1605. Whilst the project was to be abandoned after three years, a part remains; Popham's Eau, a 9km straight cut from the Old River Nene northeast of March to the Well Creek at Nordelph. Because he adopted the principle of constructing and maintaining watercourses in return for land, he was hated by the poor in Fenland and was described to King James as the 'covetous and bloodie Popham'.

Neither he nor Bishop Morton had fully grasped the concept that whilst straight watercourses would undoubtedly lead the water away faster, fen drainage needed to be considered on a regional and not local scale. Sir Robert Bevill recognised this and he put forward proposals, later to be adopted by Sir Cornelius Vermuyden, which included a new straight river from Earith to Welney and beyond.

In 1630 a group of landowners approached Francis 4th Earl of Bedford who owned some 8,100ha of land around Thorney and Whittlesey, to drain the whole of southern Fenland in return for 38,500ha (95,000 acres) of land. Of this 16,200ha (40,000 acres) were to be taxed to meet ongoing costs, 4,900ha (12,000 acres) were allocated to the King and the remaining 17,400ha (43,000 acres) were for the investors. Thirteen businessmen, five of whom were local, known as Adventurers, because they adventured their capital, joined the Earl and they appointed Sir Cornelius Vermuyden under somewhat ambiguous terms but which he understood were to make summer farming reliable and to prevent serious (but not all) winter flooding.

Between 1631 and 1637, amidst much vehement local opposition, Vermuyden improved many existing drains including Morton's Leam and built Bevill's Leam which ran for 16km from Whittlsey Mere to Guyhirn and the now extinct Peakirk Drain which ran from Peterborough also to Guyhirn. His major work however was the Bedford River completed in 1637 and which ran in a straight line from a new sluice at Earith to another new sluice at Salter's Lode near Denver and shortened the Ely–Littleport route by about 20km.

In 1637 the works, which had cost about £200,000 were adjudged to have been completed within the terms of reference. Within a year however the decision was reversed. The Adventurers received only 16,200ha (40,000 acres) and the King, in return for 23,050ha (57,000 acres), became an Adventurer with the intent of gaining year-round farming. Whilst the works were to be put in hand immediately, they were interrupted in 1642 by the Civil War.

After the war in 1649, a new Drainage Act required William, the 5th Earl and 1st Duke of Bedford, together with the original and new Venturers, to make the lands support year-round farming. A year later Vermuyden was once again appointed as Director of Works. For administrative purposes he divided the Fens into three regions; the North Level between the River Glen and Morton's Leam, the Middle Level between Morton's Leam and the Bedford River and the South Level to the south and east of the Bedford River.

Once again earlier works were repaired, banks raised and strengthened and new channels and sluices built. In the Middle Level these included the Twenty Foot River (a much improved northern part of Bevill's Leam), the Forty Foot Drain or Vermuyden's Drain lying between Ramsey and Welches Dam on the Bedford River and the Sixteen Foot Drain or Thurlow's Drain running northeast from the Forty Foot Drain near Chatteris to Popham's Eau. Although not strictly in the Middle Level, the most significant works were the cutting of a new river, the Hundred Foot Drain or New Bedford River running parallel to the first (now Old) Bedford River with a new sluice at Denver and great Barrier Banks along the outer banks of the two Bedford Rivers. Thus upland water could not only be conveyed directly to Denver, but in times of flood additional water could flow through the sluices in the Old Bedford River and instead of spreading over the neighbouring fenland, flood onto the vast reservoir, 2,270ha, lying between the two Barrier Banks.

The works were completed by 1652 and it was accepted that the aims had been achieved. The 38,500ha were finally shared out; small recompense to some who had been made virtually bankrupt by the cost of all the works, about £500,000. Vermuyden died in 1677, but his administrative boundaries, drains, rivers and banks remain today as his testament.

The Middle Level today

The Middle Level was shaped by the 17th-century drainers. Whilst the old rivers have all but vanished, their drains now flow high above the low-lying fenland in embanked channels. It is a land of contrasts. Often lonely and desolate, it has a unique beauty and awe. The landscape is flat and low-lying, interspersed with 'islands' and thriving historic market towns and villages. It is crisscrossed with straight drains and straight roads which have sudden right-angled bends. Modern electric pumps with sophisticated controls housed in low brick buildings have replaced gas engines, steam engines and windmills whose buildings once characterised the landscape. The skyscape is huge; blue skies with unbroken sunshine can contrast with spectacular thunderstorms or winter snow clouds. It can be roasting in the summer, sometimes still but frequently windy when the dry topsoil, often just seeded, is whipped away in 'Fen Blows'. It can be bitter in the winter with severe frosts and skating on the flooded Washes. The summers can be dry and the landscape scattered with plumes of irrigation water; winters can be wet with the dykes running bank-full, the washes flooded and the pumps running flat out. Above all however it is a hard working, hard worked, prosperous land.

The successors of the Commissions of Sewers are now the Middle Level Commissioners, and within the Commissioners' area are a number of Internal Drainage Boards, who provide a local flood protection service. Each are empowered to make bylaws, raise money and carry out works to maintain, improve and construct drainage and flood defence works. Whilst they are autonomous, they are subject to the overall supervision of the Environment Agency, which also owes its origins to the Commissions of Sewers.

Whilst all the drainage works have enabled the rich peats and silts to be agriculturally exploited, they may ironically lead to the demise of the fenland as we know it. Draining and successive intensive farming have lowered the original land levels by many metres such that much of the land lies well below sea level and indeed some of the soils are nearly worked out. Flood protection as opposed to land drainage has become dominant. When combined with further increases in sea level relative to the land levels, gradients will decrease. Bigger and stronger pumps will be needed, but will they be economically viable and will the gradients be steep enough to enable the water to then flow to the sea? It seems almost inevitable that Fenland is facing another relatively imminent inundation.

The Future

Because of drainage and agricultural exploitation, the Fens are still shrinking. Since the Holme Fen posts were first installed the land level has dropped by well over 4m. Although this rate of shrinkage has decreased, East Anglia continues to sink seawards and sea levels continue to rise. Whilst the rate of shrinkage may continue to decrease as the fen soils become progressively thinner and closer to the underlying clays, sea levels may rise faster due to the combined consequences of the 'Greenhouse Effect'. Thus not only is sea level rising relative to the land levels but the gradient of the rivers crossing the fens to the sea is decreasing.

Throughout the river basins feeding the fenland rivers, industrial and residential developments continue, increasing paved areas and feeding more water faster into the rivers. Increasingly efficient agricultural drainage has a similar effect. All this water has to find its way to the sea over land which is below sea level, in rivers whose gradients are decreasing and whose flood plains have been reduced in area because of development.

Consequently the emphasis on which works on rivers and sea defences are based has shifted from enabling improvements in agricultural practice to flood protection. Presently in East Anglia some £55m per year are spent to maintain, improve and construct flood defences. There may however be limits, both practical and economic, to the extent to which flood defence standards can be raised.

For example it may no longer be practical to continue raising flood banks without carrying out expensive and extensive works to improve their foundations. Equally it might be simply not economically worthwhile.

The 1947 flood, described at the time by the Catchment Board's Chief Engineer as 'by far the greatest and most sudden in living memory. It may well have been the greatest flood since the fens were first drained', became another 'measuring stick'. Substantial improvements to flood defences and, most importantly, flood forecasting and flood warning, followed. The great tragic tidal floods of 1953 demonstrated the vulnerability of East Anglia to flooding and was the catalyst for yet more works, including the flood protection works around the edge of the fens, proposed some three hundred years earlier by Cornelius Vermuyden.

Since these floods there have been greater river flows and higher water levels, however, in the fens damage has been comparatively minor and there has been no loss of life. Nevertheless the 1998 Easter floods, which caused loss of life and much damage in the upper reaches of the rivers crossing Fenland, demonstrated that there is no room for complacency. Throughout history rivers have flooded onto their natural flood plains; they will continue to do so and had development not taken place there, the consequences of the floods would have been entirely different.

With increasing knowledge, attitudes are changing and there is a realisation that rather than to continue to fight nature, it is far better to work with her. Even this approach however has its limits and nature could ultimately win. Indeed the Board of Agriculture said in 1925 that Fenland could 'return to primeval conditions'. If that should happen, whilst the circle would be complete, the wheel would still be turning and Fenland would eventually emerge again.

Acknowledgements

Grateful acknowledgement is given to all those in the Middle Level Commissioners, in the Environment Agency, in the country, in marinas, on boats, at locks, on footpaths, in tourist offices, in libraries, in museums and in churches who have all given invaluable help and encouragement to the author.

Index

Note: Page numbers in bold refer to maps

Angle Bridge, 9, 10, **12**, **21**, **22**, 23, 26, **28**, 43, 51
Angle Corner, **22**, 23, **28**
Ashline Lock, 9, 10, **12**, **22**, 19, 24
Associated British Ports, 6, 9

Back River (Drain), **24**, **25**
Beggar's Bridge, **28**
Benwick, 6, 10, 29, 30, **32**, 50, 51, 52
Bevill's Leam, 10, **12**, **22**, 23, **28**, **30**, **40**, **41**, 43, 53
Bill Fen Marina, 9, 10, 39, **41**
Black Ham, 10, 30, **40**, 43
Black Horse Drain, 51
boat registration, 7
Bodsey Farm Bridge, 39, **41**
books and maps, 8
Botany Bay Farm & Bridge, **21**, 23, 51
bridges, 9, 10
Briggate River, 9, **12**, **22**, 24, 51
Burnthouse Bridge, 10, **21**, 23

Car Dyke, 50, 52
Chainbridge, 26, **27**
Chatteris, 29, **30**, 38, 50, 53
Christchurch, 19, 52
'Cock Up' Bridge, 18
Connington Fen & Bridge, **40**, 42
Copalder Corner, 29, **32**
Curf Bridge, **33**

Delph, River & Bridge, **31**, 35, 36, 38, 39
Denver Sluice, 6, 8, **13**, **14**, **15**, 37, 38, 52, 53-4
distances & dimensions, 9-10
Dog in a Doublet, 6
Downham West, **37**
Duncombe's Bridge, **28**
Dunham's Wood, 19

Earith, 7, 9, 26, **30**, 50, 52, 53
Ely, 7, 9, 22, 24, 51, 52
Ely Marine Ltd, 9
Environment Agency, 4, 6, 7, 54
Exhibition Bridge, 10, **40**

Fenland District Council, 4, 5, 6
Field's End Bridge, 9, **24**, 26
Five Arch Bridge, **40**
Flood's Ferry, 9, 10, 11, **12**, **21**, 23, 29, **30**, **32**, 51
Forty Foot Drain, 10, 29, **30**-1, **32**-5, 38, 53
Fox Narrowboats, 9, 10, **21**, 23

Grand Union Canal, 4, 7
Great Ouse Boating Association, 4, 7, 9
Great Ouse, River, 5, 6-7, 8, 9, 10, **13**, **14**, **30**, **31**
Great Raveley Drain, 10, **40**, 42
Greenwich Meridian, 23
Herbert's Bridge, 10, **40**, 43
Hereward Way, 19, 23, 26

Hermitage Marina, 9
High Lode, 39, **41**
Hobb's Lot Bridge, 26, **27**
Holloway's Bridge, **27**
Holme Fen & posts, **30**, 39, **40**, 42, 43, 54
Horseway Bridge & Lock, 5, 10, 11, 29, **31**, **34**, 38
Horsey Bridge, **24**, **25**, 26
Hundred Foot Drain *see* New Bedford River

Infields Bridge, 10, **27**

King's Dyke, 9, 11, **12**, **24**, 26, 51
King's Lynn, 6, 7, 8, 9, 52, 53

Leonard Childs' Bridge, 29, **33**
Littleport, 7, 45, 51, 52
locks, 4, 9, 10
Lode's End Lock, 11, 29, **30**, 39, **41**, 42
Low Corner, 10, **17**, 19, **20**

Manea, **31**, 38-9
March, 8, 11, **13**, **17**, 19-23, **20**-1, 51, 52
marinas, 9, 39
Marmont Priory Lock, 9, 11, **13**, **17**, 19, **20**
Middle Level Commissioners, 5, 7, 11, 54, 55
Middle Level Main Drain, 7, 9, 11, **13**, 17, 18, 19
Monk's Lode, 10, **40**, 42, 43
mooring, 4, 5, 7
Morton's Leam, **12**, **24**, 53
Mullicourt Aqueduct, 9, **16**, 18, 19

navigation, 5, 6
Nene, River, 6, 7, 8, 9, 11, **12**, 19, **25**, 50-1, 52
    Old Course, 9, 10, 11-26, **12**, **17**, **20**-1, 29, **30**, **32**, 38, 39-42, 43, 51, 53
New Bedford River, 6, 7, **13**, **14**, **31**, 35-7, 38, 39, 50, 53-4
New Cut, 10, **30**, **40**, 43
New Dyke, 10, **30**, **40**, 42-3
Nightingale's Corner, 10, **40**, 42, 43
Nordelph, 9, 11, **15**, 17-18, 19, 52, 53
    Pipe & Bridge, 9, **15**

Old Bedford Barrier Banks, **35**, 38, 53-4
    River, 5, 10, 11, **13**, **14**, 29, **31**, 35-7, 38, 39, 54
    Sluice & Bridge, 10, 11, **13**, **14**, 29, **35**-7, 39
Oundle Marina, 9
Ouse Washes, **35**, 38, 39
Outwell, 5, 9, 11, **13**, **16**, 17-19, 51, 52

Papworth's Bridge, **41**, 42
Peterborough, 6, 7, 8, 9, **12**, **25**, 52
Peterborough Boating Centre, 9, 26
Pig Water, 26, 51
Pole's Bridge, **40**
Pondersbridge, **40**, **41**, 42

Popes Corner, 7, 9, 51
Popes Corner Marina, 9
Popham's Eau, 9, 10, **13**, **15**, 17, 18-19, **20**, 38, 53
Puddock Bridge, 10, 29
pump-out facilities, 9
Purls Bridge, **35**, 38-9

Ramsey, 29, **30**, 39-42, **41**
    Forty Foot, **32**, **33**, **41**
    High Lode, 9, 10
    Mere, 50, 51
    St Mary, **41**, 42, 51
Reed Fen Farm, 19, 26
Relief Channel Lock, **13**, **14**, **37**
Roman Fen Causeway, **17**, 22

Salter's Lode Lock, 5, 7, 9, 10, 11, 38, 53
Shepperson's Bridge, 19, 26, **27**
Sixteen Foot Drain, 10, **17**, 18, 19, **31**, **34**, 38, 53
speed limits, 10
Sovereign Quarter Horses, 26
Speed the Plough Bridge, **40**, 42
Staffurth's Bridge, 9, **21**, 23, 51
Stanground, 8, **24**, **25**, 26, 51, 52, 53
    Lock, 5, 7, 9, 11, **12**, **25**, 26
Stonea, 19
Stuntney, 51
Sutton Bridge, 6

Tebbitt's Bridge, **40**
telephone numbers, 9
Three Holes, 6, 10, 17, 18, 19, 38
Thurlow's Drain *see* Sixteen Foot Drain
tides, 6-7
tourist information, 9
Turningtree Bridge, **22**, 23
Twenty Foot River, 9, 10, 19, **12**, 23, 26, **27**, **28**, 53

Ugg Mere, **40**, 42, 51
Upwell, 9, 11, **13**, **16**, 17, **17**, 18-19, **20**, 38, 51, 52, 53
Upwood, **40**, **41**

Vermuyden's Drain *see* Forty Foot Drain

Welches Dam Lock, 5, 10, 11, 29, **31**, **35**, 38, 53
Well Creek, 9, 11, **13**, **14**, **15**, **16**, 52, 53
    Trust & Nature Trail, 4, 11, 17
Wells Bridge, 10, 29, **30**, **32**, **33**, 39, **41**
Welmore Lake Sluice, **37**, 38
Welney, **31**, **36**, 39, 51, 53
West View Marina, 9
White Fen Farm Bridge, 10, **32**
White House Farm Bridge, 9
Whittlesey, 9, 10, **12**, 19, **22**, **24**, 24-6, 52, 53
    Dyke, 9, 10, **12**, **21**, 23, 26, 51
    Mere, **40**, 43, 51, 52, 53
Wisbech, 6, 8, 51, 52
Wisbech Canal, 17, 18
Wissey Bridge, **13**
Woodwalton Fen, **40**, 42

Yaxley, **40**, 42, 43
Yaxley Lode, **40**, 43, 51